MW01026267

Becoming a Complete
Martial Artist

Becoming a Complete
Martial Artist

Error Detection in Self-Defense and the Martial Arts

Tristan Sutrisno and Marc MacYoung

with Dianna Gordon

THE LYONS PRESS
Guilford, Connecticut
An imprint of The Globe Pequot Press

The Lyons Press is an imprint of The Globe Pequot Press.

10 9 8 7 6 5 4 3 2 1

Printed in the United States of America

Designed by Stephanie Doyle

Photos by Marc MacYoung, Tristan Sutrisno, Dianna Gordon,
Jessie Alcorta, Page Alcorta, Doug Witrock, John Hannigan.

Library of Congress Cataloging-in-Publication Data

Sutrisno, Tristan
    Becoming a complete martial artist: error detection in self-defense and the
martial arts / by Tristan Sutrisno and Marc MacYoung with Dianna Gordon.
    p. cm.
ISBN 1-59228-370-5 (trade cloth)
1.   Martial arts-Training. 2. Self-defense. I. MacYoung, Marc. II. Gordon,
Dianna. III. Title.

GV1102.7.T7S87 2004
613.7'148-dc22

2004048829

To my wife Dianna Gordon MacYoung

—M. M.

To my dad

—T. S.

Contents

Acknowledgments

I am indebted to all wonderful people who have impacted my life and helped me in writing this book. I am so grateful to:

My Dad and Pak Lek, for showing me everything they could about martial arts. And for demonstrating that spiritual and temporal leadership are not mutually exclusive.

My coauthors Marc and Dianna for showing me that searing brilliance, passionate conviction, and gentle persuasion can go hand in hand.

Gerry Scheila, for his friendship and valuable contribution to the preparation of this book.

Howard Cox, MD, a former Army Ranger, Vietnam veteran, Distinguished Service Cross awardee, for showing me that you don't have to have the same mother to be brothers.

Mike Higgins, former Marine Recon Force pilot, Vietnam veteran, Distinguished Air Service awardee, for showing me the map of life, courage, and friendship.

Jack Finch, former intelligence officer, veteran of Vietnam, Grenada, and Desert Storm, Silver Star recipient, for showing me how to forgive when faced with the unforgivable and allowing me to move on with my life.

Peter Whitehouse: Ron Holloway; Don Gladfelter; Mike Kush, DDS; Joe Piro; Bill Wertman; Mike Dennison; Scott Ivory; Greg Olande; Scott Watson; and the rest of the Bushi No Te members for demonstrating what discipline, loyalty, and unwavering commitment are all about.

Ed Fanning, Montie, Mama Duck, Slugg, Da Bean, Martin, Doug, Terry, Barry, Pancho, Drew, and the rest of the Animal List members for their lasting friendship and valuable suggestions, insights, and opinions.

My daughters Angelique, Marissa, Trisha, Jacqueline, and Tristan for their unwavering love, compassion, and care, the importance of family, and the importance of being there.

Most of all, Mary Beth Sunick, Ph. D., for showing me that when humans are willing to love, there is no limit to what can compassionately be created and gently overlooked.

For any good thing that may come from me, most of it comes from them. For they have taught it to me and I have merely passed it on.

Tristan Sutrisno

Many words in this book stem from our wonderful relationship with the members of Animal List for their wit, empathy, compassion, intelligence, and constant thirst for knowledge. May they always keep us on our toes.

We are indebted to Jesse and Page Alcorta for fine photographic work and many late night conversations, hashing out the fine points of teaching and the martial arts. And especially to Jesse, who made a fine uke for Tristan and photo model for portions of this book. To John Hannigan and Doug Wittrock who provided fun and valuable insights during the photo sessions for this book.

And most of all to Tristan, who is our friend and our teacher. A compassionate and caring man whose students are the most fortunate in the world to have him as sensei.

Acknowledgments

And to all our students, who continue to teach us every time we step onto the dojo floor or through the door of the coffee shop.

And to all who have gone before us, leaving a legacy and wealth of knowledge we gratefully attempt to communicate to the best of our abilities.

Marc and Dianna Gordon MacYoung

Precedence Is No Excuse for Failure

This book is not about how we are right, and everyone else is wrong.

This book is about fixing "errors" in the way people do the martial arts. By errors, we mean extraneous details that have crept in or elements that have been omitted that rob you of effectiveness. Individually these elements are small and seemingly insignificant, but collectively they are critical.

We offer you a book about diagnostics. If you can't identify the problem, you can't fix it. First we'll give you the standards and process to diagnose your martial art movement. Then we'll give you the tools to fix the errors that have crept in. It doesn't matter what style you practice; you can apply these diagnostics.

This book is not about the "right way" to do something; it is about getting the job done. There is a very good chance that the problem is not you doing the technique incorrectly. The technique itself may have decayed to the point where it is no longer effective. It doesn't matter that you perform a technique perfectly if that technique has been changed over time to the point it doesn't work. Important concepts have been lost over time as the system moved further away from the intent of the original founder or founders. It has reached the point where errors are being taught as the "right way" to do a move.

We offer no excuses, no rationalizations, no long-winded dissertations about how ancient or traditional a move is and that is why you must do it this particular way. We simply ask: Does it work as advertised? Do your blocks keep you from getting hit? Do your attacks deliver force? If not, why not?

That takes it out of the realm of who's right or wrong and puts it into the land of effectiveness.

Being a complete martial artist isn't about being right; it's about being effective—no matter what style or variation you do. Different schools, even in the same style, do things slightly differently. They often engage in ferocious arguments over which variation is the "right" way to do a technique. Arguing who is right or wrong or over variations of a style is exactly the kind of thinking that has led to the martial arts problems this book addresses.

Let's look at blocks as an example. The purpose of a block is *to keep from being hit*. If it doesn't meet this fundamental criteria, something is wrong. It doesn't matter which variation of a block is "right," there is a problem if you are getting hit half the time. This tends to happen because each variation is designed to handle the style of punching used in a particular school. In evolving to handle a specific type of punch, a block can lose general elements that make it effective. As long as you are attacked with a specific punch, you won't get hit. When it's another variation, then odds are your block will not work.

When you teach a doubtful technique to students, and you authorize the student to teach that same doubtful technique, sooner or later, the student has to improvise and "patch" with speed or muscle to make it work. That is assuming you haven't patched it in this manner already.

This book appears at a time when public discussion of the Asian martial arts phenomenon has been made possible by teachers traveling to other countries from Asia and by the so-called grand masters or masters in the United States and Europe. This holds true for the authors, too, who come from both Eastern and Western heritages, as well as radically different martial arts backgrounds.

We expect this book to be controversial.

First, it is written by nonmasters of the arts. Although collectively the authors and editor of this book have more than a hundred years of experience in the martial arts and fighting, we do not claim to be masters. What we know is nothing in comparison to how much is left to learn. We refuse to be called "masters," "gurus," "shihans," "dai-sifus," or "soke-dais." In fact, even if we have been at it much longer than most so-called masters, we still consider ourselves to be students trying to understand the simplest of moves. By the end of this book, you will understand why we focus on these fundamentals.

Second, this book challenges established opinions and concepts. These myths of the martial arts are usually not questioned in the cold, hard light of practicality. Can this move perform what it is supposed to do? If it doesn't, then either something is wrong with the move or the interpretation of what it's for is incorrect. Unfortunately, a lot of people have quite a bit invested in these questionable interpretations.

Third, and perhaps the most important, this book exposes gaps in the progression of techniques that many martial arts students wonder about, but don't have the knowledge to phrase as penetrating questions when facing the master. Nor do they have the background to analyze the technique's explanation to see if it is feasible.

You are going to see one phrase used constantly in this book: "one, two, three, . . . nine, ten." What we mean is that too many instructors and students want to jump from fundamentals and basics (one, two, three) to the fun stuff of advanced techniques (. . . nine, ten). What the instructors have lost and their students will not get and the students of those students will never know, is that "four, five, six, seven, and eight" are what make the system effective.

This book will expose issues that people, who are listed as masters on paper, really might not want you to know. These "paper masters" have documents all over their walls proclaiming their mastery of a martial art style, but they've been promoted so quickly that they've had little time to absorb or study the fundamental principles underlying their styles. As such, they don't want you knowing or asking about certain things because it will reveal the gaps in their understanding.

Having said this, however, we have tried to communicate the ideas in a manner that open-minded martial arts practitioners can see and comprehend. Our goal is to help you grow in your style. This book will also be of great value to instructors in teaching. You will find many useful terms and ideas to assist you in communicating critical components to your students.

So let's begin: How did these errors creep into the martial arts?

Long before servicemen returned from the occupation of Japan and long before Bruce Lee, Chuck Norris, et al., popularized the martial arts with American audiences, there were long traditions of fighting styles, sometimes village or family arts, handed down within small, select populations.

As the arts were taught by founder to master to instructor to student, who then became an instructor, they have encountered a common human condition. That is, as each teacher hands an art to a student, there are subtle, often unremarked, deviations from the founder's original idea or intent.

Humans, being what they are, will tend to emphasize the things that best fit their physiology and strengths. The fast person will emphasize speed a bit more because it fits with what he or she can do well. The strong man or woman will emphasize muscle over other aspects because it is something he or she has been successful using. Students will gravitate to a certain set of techniques or principles they find uniquely fit them. As they become teachers, it's only human to place a bit more emphasis on these personally popular applications.

So in every art through history, there have been minute changes: things forgotten, things lost, things modified, things changed. In that process, there have been aspects whose origins and purposes were well known to the founder, but that are a mystery to a tenth-generation student because they have been inadvertently lost from the system.

Enter popularity spurred by Hollywood and the advent of commercial and sport martial arts. As school owners jockeyed for tournament trophies and dollars, the pace of evolution of these fighting arts from village- and family-based systems to other American applications quickened. There was a rush to "get to the good stuff," and many changes were made. Not all of them were oriented on effective power delivery or handling the same from your opponent. Often these changes were predicated on increased success in the faster, less violent, sports ring.

Although training for a different intent and purpose, practitioners told themselves that they were still training for the original. In time, some martial arts became similar to trying to outfit a hockey team in baseball uniforms. Hockey equipment is designed for a specific activity and to protect the player. But it takes time to put it on. In the rush to advance in a system or style, it became easier to don the lighter, faster, easier-to-wear "gear" of summer to get players into the game.

In the transition, some of the equipment needed for protection on the ice would be discarded. In time, it would evolve to where new students never learned certain equipment ever existed, much less how to use it. This occurs with players thinking they are playing the original game. The same is true with martial arts.

If errors have crept into a move, you may never know because you can always think the problem is with you. This can happen when there is no feedback from outside sources. If a move fails to achieve its objective, it is easy for a student to say, "I did it wrong." Unfortunately, this tendency is encouraged by teachers who have managed to somehow patch the flawed move. This sort of instructor tends to blame the system's performance failure on the student. We cannot begin to tell you the number of times we have heard instructors say to students when a technique fails, "You did it wrong." No, the student did exactly what he or she was taught; it was the move that was flawed.

In time, this failure becomes acceptable. Teachers and students can accept something filled with small errors as the correct way to execute a move. Since students don't expect more than, for example, a 30 percent success rate, they accept it as normal. They just assume they did the technique wrong 70 percent of the time when it didn't work as advertised. Instructors, through diligent practice, might be able to up their success rate to 75 percent. But the technique's tendency to fail is still present.

In the dojo, a system's or technique's failure doesn't usually result in serious injury to the student or instructor. But how would you like to try these same odds of success against a 250-pound biker on PCP? Or during a knife attack? That is not the opportune time to discover there may be flaws in your training.

The primary question isn't: Am I doing it right? If "right" means to you "Am I doing it exactly as instructed?" That's a secondary question. The primary questions are: What am I doing correctly? How do you know it works? Does a move meet its stated objective? If a move has multiple applications, do you know them all?

This failure to perform has led many to seek the ultimate martial art, or reality-based fighting. Others seek to solve the problem through cross-training. What few people realize is that these other systems are just as riddled with errors. These errors are different, but they are often as numerous. Although there will be holes filled with cross-training, you don't solve problems by finding a new set of errors. You solve them by finding the original errors in your preferred style and correcting them. This isn't to say you should not cross-train, but, rather, if you do, you should seek the same level of understanding in all your arts. You should continue to build a solid structure with an established foundation and not simply erect multiple, flawed foundations. This leads to a depth of understanding; not just a wide, but shallow, knowledge of the martial arts.

The goal of this book is to put back some of the missing pieces by looking at a generic hard-style martial art, finding the holes via error detection, and giving you, the reader, the elements to plug these leaks. We are not claiming that this is the right way to do things. What we are trying to show is how you can apply error detection to whatever style you practice and start fixing lapses that might have crept in. Although we demonstrate with a hard style, the general concepts can be applied to any martial art.

This book is mainly about helping everyone achieve their goals. But first you have to define the goal; then it defines you. Defining a goal will guide you in knowing what you wish to accomplish. Absent such knowledge, enter neither fight nor battle.

Read on, learn, and enjoy. We hope this book excites, inspires, and helps you in your growth as a martial artist.

—Sutrisno, MacYoung, and Gordon

— 1 —

What Is Error Detection?

Fundamentals versus Basics

Let's begin by defining the difference between "basic" and "fundamental." Many martial arts schools do not make this critical distinction, and it is the source of major confusion.

A fundamental is a concept or idea that a system arises from and rests upon. It is a foundation. Fundamentals by their nature are simple, but profound. They are primary, but capable of incredibly subtle and complex manifestations. A fundamental can be exhibited in hundreds of different techniques. One such fundamental is the skill of weight transfer. It is something so simple that its study is often overlooked. Yet without a firm understanding of this fundamental, you will not be able to generate power.

A basic is an introduction. It is a starting point where a student can become aware not only of fundamentals, but also of how things are done in a particular style. If fundamentals are the foundation, then basics are the front door. They are the first things you are taught when you enter a system. In a perfect world, basics and fundamentals are the same.

More commonly though, basics are teaching tools to introduce the student to what makes up a style. It is in this meaning
that errors begin to creep in. You cannot learn a fundamental
without learning a basic. You can, however, be taught the basics
without being taught fundamentals. For example, a student can
be taught the "basics," such as front stance, down block, punch,
and front snap kick without being taught the fundamentals of
those actions: efficient elbow position and body movement for
blocking, range, correct structure, motion and timing for
punches, proper weight transfer for kicks and stances.

Fundamentals must be present for a move to work. Lacking
fundamentals, these same basics often become shallow reflec-
tions of the originals. They don't work by themselves; they
require either the addition of all kinds of other bells and whis-
tles or are dropped from the student's attempts to apply the art.
(Think about it, when was the last time you saw someone in a
front stance during a sparring match?) This, despite the instructor's insistence that the student must return to the basics. But
why should he? What the student knows as the basics don't
work. Not knowing the fundamentals, students often convince
themselves that the secrets of success are in the advanced, more
complicated techniques, when in fact, success stems from knowing how to apply the fundamentals in *any* technique. When you
can do this, even basic moves work effectively.

If you do not learn the fundamentals through your basics,
your system will not work. This is a problem because many
people want to rush past the basics and get to the "good stuff."
In their mind, effectiveness comes from knowing advanced
techniques. One, two, three, . . . nine, ten. They skip the middle part, which is where they would come to understand the
fundamentals.

What Is Error Detection?

The history of American martial arts is replete with examples of people who went to the Orient, obtained a ranking of something akin to yellow or green belt, and came back to the United States as a "fifth-degree black belt." We suspect there is some invisible line much like the international dateline; when a martial artist crosses it, this magical transformation to fifth degree occurs. Unfortunately, as anyone who has been involved with international organizations can tell you, the blame for this situation is not entirely with American and European martial artists.

Even if a person has been training others for twenty-five years since his time in the Orient, what has he been teaching? How much time has he spent reinventing the wheel? Or, more commonly, how much "patching" has he done, to cover the holes in his knowledge? What did he put in that allowed a technique to work for him? Often the answer is speed or muscle. This lack of knowledge manifests in his teaching. One, two, three, . . . nine, ten. These instructors never knew what they missed because their systems never followed a circle of always coming back to fundamentals and basics for further depth and exploration.

There also is the issue of a student becoming an instructor and stopping learning. A person could well say he or she has been in the martial arts for twenty, thirty, or forty years, but the bulk of that could well have been spent teaching a specific system. This means an individual is not learning as a student, but instead is an instructor who must maintain his authority and not undermine it by taking the perceived lesser status of a pupil. Unfortunately, this results in his not learning the subject fully. Instead of comprehending the subject for what it is, he attempts to cobble it onto what he already knows. One, two, three . . . nine, ten.

Effectiveness, at any level, comes from knowing the fundamentals and making sure they are present in whatever technique you do. It is the rush to get past the basics that results in overlooked fundamentals. But without the fundamentals, the moves just don't work in reality, even though they look really flashy. This results in a situation where the martial artist is stuck with the gates down, the lights flashing, but no train coming.

Why Do We Need to Review Our Martial Art Style?

With the awareness of the differences between basics and fundamentals, we would like you to consider the following statement: *one martial arts fundamental is the weak against the strong.*

It's a simple concept, but one that can have many meanings and interpretations—and you can find thousands of different manifestations. When we speak of it here, we are referring to the interpretation that the martial arts are designed to overcome disadvantages and turn them into advantages. They teach the weak to defend themselves against the strong by using other forces, such as leverage, placement, and gravity. By skillfully utilizing these more reliable forces, strength becomes a secondary issue. The need for error detection is evident if you accept this simple premise of weakness overcoming strength. You cannot overcome strength if you cannot control the fundamentals that can counter it.

As a gross generalization, *Western fighters work at becoming strong, while techniques become secondary.*

Through superior technique, you may neutralize superior strength. That is the point that is lost with the idea of making yourself stronger. Some people want to make themselves stronger through technique, instead of realizing that proper technique neutralizes strength. They try to make their technique strong (or fast), instead of correct. This goes against the fundamental of the weak vying successfully against the strong.

People who are either strong or fast can compensate for a lack of fundamentals with their natural abilities, and through practice can refine these natural attributes. Even though they are not doing the technique "correctly," it still works for them because of these compensatory elements. To their perception, it works, therefore it must be correct. It's not mastery; it's sheer, raw, physical attributes that make it work.

It is here that errors begin to creep in. These people cannot teach what they themselves don't know. They omit critical components that would make it work for other, less athletically endowed people. Since they never had to learn these components, their students are not likely to discover them on their own. Simply stated, you cannot learn things that you cannot imagine.

An example of this is found in a particular kata—Heian 3 (Japanese) or Pyong 3 (Korean). After a spear hand to the solar plexus, the person performing the kata envisions that the wrist of the spear hand is grabbed and does a back turn to a horse stance. This supposedly creates a hand escape, while the kata performer fires off a back fist or hammer fist to the opponent.

This is how it is commonly taught. A strong man can do it, as can a small fast man, if he moves before the grip is secured. But a smaller, slower person can't.

Such a person would literally twist his arm behind his back and still stay in the opponent's grip. Without the release of the grip, the person trying this move has literally put himself into a joint lock. The other person, by simply lifting the kata performer's arm, would destroy the strike's effectiveness. The only reason it works in the dojo is because training partners cooperate. All it takes is a strong training partner cranking down his grip, and the problems with this idea become blatantly obvious.

It would be easy at this moment to dismiss this move altogether. But just because the error-riddled version does not work (or only works for the strong and fast) does not mean that the move doesn't work—especially when all the component parts are present.

Those parts are: from the spear hand, pull back and reverse the grip. Now, instead of him grabbing your wrist, you are grabbing his. From that new position, body pivot pulls him off balance and right into your fist.

That simple reversal of a grip is a prime example of a 4, 5, 6, 7, 8 issue that has been lost. It is a common error in how this move is both taught and explained. Without this practical element—which changes everything—there are still many people who believe that the original move would work to free them from a grab by an uncooperative opponent. Why shouldn't they? Even though they can't do it yet, they have seen sensei do it.

Detecting Errors

Detecting and correcting errors is one of the most difficult skills to achieve in learning martial arts (or any sport). To detect errors, you must first comprehend the fundamentals. You then focus on one technique to recognize its purpose and the body mechanics involved, and clearly understand its advantages and disadvantages. To do this, you have to analyze it—based on reality, not fantasy.

PYONG

Spear hand.

Break grip.

Turn.

Back fist.

<u>WHAT HAPPENS WITH PYONG 3</u>

Spear hand.

Attempt to break grip.

WHAT HAPPENS WITH PYONG 3 *(continued)*

Cross step.

Countered!

An example of this is questioning an off-angle kick in a kata when your last move was oriented on an opponent right in front of you. In situations like this, it is not uncommon for a third move to return to the original line. The frequent explanation for the 45-degree-angle kick is that you are fighting multiple opponents. You block one attack from the first in front, kick the second, and then return your attention to the first.

One must realistically wonder, however, why the original attacker conveniently stands there waiting for you to kick his friend without launching another attack. Is it us or does it seem that the people telling this story are expecting cooperative attackers? Yet this and similar explanations are not only readily

HEIAN KATA

Spear hand.

HEIAN KATA *(continued)*

Weight transfer/reverse grip.

Back fist.

accepted but are, in fact, embedded in the mind of the student—who later becomes a teacher.

Now we must admit that many of these errors are not the fault of the teacher. In fact, most instructors are, in good faith, passing on what they were taught. What they fail to understand is how what they were taught has been influenced by sports trends, martial arts fads, nationalistic changes (i.e., taking a style from another country, changing it, and claiming it is indigenous), or individuals and organizations making up forms and claiming they are traditional. Most instructors have obtained information through martial arts sources and haven't compared those data against historical, anthropological, or cultural sources or taken political influences into consideration. All of this has significantly shaped the martial arts.

Error detection is one of the most advanced skills a martial artist can learn and the most humbling of experiences—yet is essential for all instructors. It takes sophisticated expertise to look at the total technique and determine the presence of an error and what to do about it. Error detection comes through analyzing and determining the technique's many objectives and making sure that all the component parts are present to achieve its goals. If a move is explained as a throw, then all of the elements of a throw must be there. Otherwise the explanation and application of the move are bunk.

Many different methods work, which is something really fun to discover. Be careful, however, not to overload your students with too many techniques before the fundamentals are understood. You cannot pile technique upon technique and hope that students will discover the fundamentals through diversity. You must teach the fundamentals and assist students to explore the application and effectiveness of what they already know before you start piling on more techniques. We will be the first to admit that many commercial schools use this "piling on" strategy to maintain student interest; unfortunately, what results is a wide knowledge of techniques, but a severe weakness in executing them and a shallowness of understanding.

Take your time and help your students explore the depth of each technique within the kata. Do not rush or allow the student to hurry past the fundamentals. When you do that, errors creep in. Every day, help them discover new and exciting truths about what they already know and how it can be applied. Being a complete martial artist is about understanding and being able to make what you know work, not having several thousand moves that you do poorly. What's more, by taking this attitude you significantly lessen the likelihood of black belt burnout. There is no reaching the apex and then becoming bored because "you know it all;" growth in fundamentals is a never-ending adventure and challenge.

Next to rushing through techniques, the most common error in trying to keep student interest is trying to explain everything about a particular technique before all the fundamentals are in place. Explaining too much too soon often results in mental indigestion, especially for beginners. First, focus on gross body movement and explanation and demonstration of the fundamentals contained therein. Teach details later.

Do not attempt to tell your students everything that you know or the myriad possible applications of a technique. Instead, focus on one or two components of the entire technique at a time and emphasize developing them. Especially focus on those elements that must be present for the move to work.

One simply cannot pay attention to a long list of details while learning. Focus on body posture, arm and leg placement, direction of body movement (weight transfer), and breathing pattern.

Too much insistence on correct performance can inhibit progress. Students will become discouraged, stop practicing, or drop out of the school. When the student has developed the ability to consistently display the component you had him focus on, then you can add another. By slowly adding those details in a progressive manner, you not only keep the student working to fully develop the technique, but you can keep it interesting, too.

Students must be able to feel their errors by comparing them with the feeling of correct techniques. You do this by initially moving the student's body into the correct position. Once learned, the student self adjusts.

When a student is moving differently from what is needed for the technique being practiced, it can help reduce student frustration if you simply indicate that the student is, in fact, doing a different technique. Moving in that manner is not wrong per se, but it is not what you are attempting to teach at the moment. This gives the student a second frame of reference, extra coordinates if you will. Instead of having to fish around in space, the student has another way of moving to compare it to.

~ 2 ~

Range, Weight Transfer, Positioning, Posture, and Placement

It is our intent to guide you to a better understanding of the Asian martial arts. This chapter will introduce the fundamentals we constantly address in this book. You cannot focus without an idea to focus upon, in the same way you can't plot a course to Sheppton, Pennsylvania, if you don't know where Sheppton is located. Once you know your goal, you can focus on getting there. Bottom line—you cannot learn martial arts if you don't know (or your teacher did not know) the fundamentals.

The problem with most failed techniques can usually be found in any of five main sources: range, weight transfer, positioning (or body movement), posture, and placement. These elements are to martial arts what the engine and transmission are to a car. They are the power source and control that make it go. Without them, you may have the form (chassis), but it isn't going anywhere.

Range

Range is the distance that can be reached by your hands or feet (or a weapon) to deliver force into your target with maximum efficiency.

Although range is important in all kinds of offense and defense, for ease of communication we will discuss it in striking terms. Range has three parts: reach, distance, and target impact point. You must know the reach of your punches, kicks, or weapons. That means how far out they go. Your arms are only so long, as are your legs. Reach is how far you can reach without sacrificing structure or balance by adding shoulder twists or leaning over to gain an extra few inches.

Distance, however, can be affected by your position and the direction you are moving. It is reach extended by movement. For example, the distance you cover from a neutral stance (weight 50/50) is the same as your reach because you are not moving your body. Whereas in a front stance, the distance you can cover will range from your reach from that stance while stationary (without shifting your weight) to the distance you can cover starting with your weight on the back foot and transferring your weight to your front foot. The weight transfer allows you to cover more distance. If you take a long step into a front stance, you greatly increase the distance you are covering. Stepping forward and kicking extends the distance even more. In each instance you have covered a different distance: short, medium, and long. The distance not only affects which tool you use, but how you adjust to achieve placement.

A target impact point is where you want to deliver the power of a move. Target impact is not just the spot on your opponent's body that you are aiming at, it also is how deeply into his body you aim your blow. If you fall short of this spot, your power won't be delivered. If you overshoot, your hit will probably become a push. There is great debate about what the "most efficient" target impact point is. Do you aim for a surface, the middle of your opponent's mass, or six inches behind his back? The answer is: it depends on the technique you are doing and what you want to achieve.

Range is a combination of reach and the distance you can cover (by transferring weight, stepping, and moving into position) to hit the target with maximum force. Understanding range is the strategic understanding of what you get when you combine weight transfer, positioning, and placement—and how to apply them in fighting.

To define your range, you have to hit the target impact point while in different stances with a full impact and use your left hand first, followed by your right hand and vice versa. It is the same with kicks and weapons. Only when you understand your reach, the distance to your target's impact point and how to cover it, will you begin to understand range.

To understand the reach of techniques, you must practice executing them as frequently as possible and from different positions or stances. To understand distance, you must practice the same using a target and covering the distance to hit with maximum force with weight transfer. Don't try to force the technique; there are some distances and positions where it just will not work. You learn as much from these failures as you do from the successes of being in the right range.

Discovering your range is finding the point where you deliver the most power with a move. The defining word here, however, is "you." Your range cannot be taught to you—you must learn it for yourself. Your instructor can guide and assist you in finding where you need to be, but only you will be able to determine your exact range. Since individual range fluctuates for different people and various body types, the best an instructor can do would be to give you a rough estimate of where you need to be to deliver maximum force efficiently.

We have spoken of range in terms of offense; however, it is also a critical component of defense. Your range sets your "defensive perimeter." All martial artists must be aware that securing their perimeter is one of the most important fighting techniques, offensively or defensively. Your perimeter must and should be protected at all times. But you will not know your perimeter until you know range.

Students need to be taught to be cognizant that wherever they move, their perimeter moves as well. You not only control your perimeter and everything within it, you also control its location. Think of your perimeter as a hula hoop; it moves with you. And that moving circle is your domain.

Students also should be aware that the counterattack is at their disposal. For example, your opponent crosses the invisible line that is your perimeter. This means you can reach him with a kick. At that time, you have three options: kick, move to the side (into positioning for another attack), or move away from the line of attack without counterattacking. Having said this, the time to recognize the potential for a counterattack is when your opponent moves into your perimeter, not when he's standing within his and your attack ranges. You do not want to let someone linger in attack range.

Good understanding of range not only works in the sparring ring, but can save your life in the real world. Knowing attack range, you do not allow a potential attacker to get close enough to be successful. Far too many attacks are successful because the victim allowed the attacker to get within range.

Although we will discuss it in more depth in the weapons chapter, a point that we would like to make is that a weapon is an extension of your hand. It is a means for you to gain more range and extend your reach. This is done, however, at the cost of hand mobility and loss of possible use for other techniques. The reason is your hand is now fixed around the weapon. We are critical of any kind of weapon as giving any advantage other than range extension or cutting.

Our opinion is: learn how to hit correctly. The advantages you might gain by hitting harder using small strike enhancers (i.e., kubotan) are counterbalanced by the disadvantages of loss of hand mobility and failure to extend range. It doesn't matter if you can hit harder than normal if you are still in range to get hit yourself.

Learning range is a critical part of learning how to hit. If you have not gained an understanding of range, you will not be able to hit hard. This is why many people want to compensate for this lack by the use of strike enhancers. Unfortunately, this is not the student's fault; often so-called instructors don't teach how important range is in enhancing techniques to successfully accomplish objectives. Instead they teach their students to put their faith in gadgets, toys, and whippy sticks. This is another example of one, two, three, . . . nine, ten.

Weight Transfer

Weight transfer is the most important part of martial arts movement. Sadly, too many instructors don't understand its importance, therefore they do not have a clear explanation nor the ability to teach it to their students. It's another case of one, two, three, . . . nine, ten and the source of many errors that have crept into martial arts training. Without weight transfer, there is no power.

Walking is an example of weight transfer. When the person is relaxed, the walk is smooth and subtle. If the person is tense, it will disturb the walking motion and he moves like a robot. Walking is taken for granted. We forget that when we were children, it took a lot of practice and falls to stand up and walk one step at a time.

Everyone knows walking, but when you power walk or if you are going to compete in a power walking contest, you have to relearn how to walk efficiently and strategically. The objective is composed of many goals or a series of steps to accomplish it. They must be concrete and identifiable milestones toward a larger target. The same can be said about learning weight transfer for the martial arts.

What few people realize is that although weight transfer is a critical component of walking, a step and weight transfer are not the same thing. You can step without transferring weight, and you can transfer weight without stepping (as in shifting your weight from foot to foot). Recognizing this difference is an important step in learning weight transfer and, by extension, effective movement.

You can practice weight management and transference with your left foot at 11 o'clock (12 o'clock is directly in front of your nose). Slowly transfer 85 percent of your body weight to the front (front stance). Slowly move your weight back and stop at the center where your body weight would be equally divided between front leg and back leg (50/50, a.k.a., finding your center). Then slowly transfer 65 percent of your weight to the back leg (finding your back stance).

The next move would be to 1 o'clock with your right foot and follow the same exercise of weight transfer. This exercise is very critical and should be practiced religiously with the left and right foot. Weight transfer is economy of motion. This method not only will help your stamina, but is also strategically sound.

This exercise also teaches the three distances—critical, offensive, and safe distance—which we will go into later. In response to a right-hand attack, however, transferring your weight to 11 o'clock is moving into safe distance; 1 o'clock is into offensive distance; moving into either 12 o'clock or toward 6 o'clock would be staying in critical distance.

To do this, weight transfers are needed that are a good combination of stances, superior judgment of distance, excellent balance, and coordination. You don't get these without specifically practicing each of them separately and in combination. In the martial arts world, a player whose survival techniques mainly depend on weight transfer movements should pay serious attention to these methods of weight management. Take the time to go back and review these fundamentals.

With weight management, you control the weight transfer in a smooth and even way so your motion doesn't stall. This is simple, but it will need a coordination of weight transfer and positioning. You must be able to smoothly flow from one placement of your weight (in a position) to another and be aware of where your weight is at all times. Without the understanding and practice of weight transfer, any movement would tense and result in slower and sloppier moves.

To give you an idea of the importance of weight transfer, we will explain it in the context of hitting. Let's say, hypothetically, that the weight transfer takes two seconds from start to finish. Your punch takes one second. To manifest your weight

PROPER WEIGHT TRANSFER

Weight on one leg.

Extend foot.

Transfer weight.

Stance.

POOR WEIGHT TRANSFER

Weight 50/50.

Shifting weight and leaning back.

Stepping and shifting weight.

Trying to find stance.

transfer in your punches, your timing must be correct. Your punch should be launched near the end of the weight transfer so everything arrives at once. You do not launch your punch at the first part of the weight transfer. That means you would hit halfway through the weight transfer. Nor do you want to launch it at the very end of the weight transfer. That would not only disconnect your weight transfer from your punch, but it would make it a three-second process (weight shift, punch). Instead, you want to launch your punch in the last half of the weight transfer, so it and weight arrive at the same time.

A similar version of the previous weight transfer exercise can be done for kicking. But instead of an 85/15 transfer, make it 100 percent. At first go slowly and make sure that all of your weight is over your supporting leg before kicking. The test to see if your weight is correct is to kick and then bring your foot back. If you find yourself teetering or counterbalancing to stay upright, you are not in balance nor is your weight exactly where it is supposed to be. You should be able to calmly "perch" on one leg like a stork.

Three important types of weight transfer in martial arts occur while:

> **Adjusting distance:** This is when you adjust or take advantage of distance by transferring your weight in the direction you will be using to establish safe, critical, offensive, or defensive distance.
>
> **Moving:** For most movements, the key to achieving successful weight transfer while moving is to keep the upper body straight and your center intact, or keep your upper body perpendicular to the center of the stance. Whether walking or twisting, this rule applies.

Establishing the direction of moves: For the sake of discussion, we assume a right-sided attack. Weight transfer is involved in the three types of moves that will benefit you in a real fight: (1) To the left side (11 o'clock), or safe distance; (2) to the right side (1 o'clock), or offensive distance; and (3) noon to noon, or defensive or critical distance, which is a very common reaction from inexperienced fighters. It's called critical distance because it leaves your body in line with your attacker. Therefore, it puts you in a high-risk situation.

This brings us to the next critical concept, positioning.

Positioning

Positioning is the art of being where you need to be to get the job done. Your objective is to maneuver to either side of your attacker (safe distance, where he cannot hit you but you can hit him), go on the offensive (close, where you can hit/kick him), or move away (retreat). You want to move to provide optimal distance (positioning) when blocking, deflecting, or counterattacking.

There are four fundamental positions: critical, defensive, safe, and offensive.

Critical Positioning

Critical distance is not a happy place. In fact, it is included only as a reference point for where you don't want to be. Unfortunately, entirely too many people try to fight from this foolish choice of positioning. Critical distance is when your opponent stands at noon, and you are on his noon. You are facing each other. The real bad news is you both are in each other's range.

The danger of critical distance can be mathematically explained. If you are faster than he is, you will hit him. If he is faster than you, he will hit you. If you are equally fast, you both will get hit. That means two out of three times, you're going to get hit. That's why it is called critical distance.

CRITICAL DISTANCE

If you are faster, you will hit your opponent.

If you are slower, you will be hit.

If you are equally fast, you will both be hit.

Defensive Positioning

Defensive distance is moving away from the firing line or from your attacker's punch by going to the side or anywhere between 9 o'clock and 3 o'clock. This buys you distance. If you choose an off angle, your opponent must take the extra time and effort to re-orient and bring you back into critical distance.

Stepping back (6 o'clock) is part of defensive distance, and this is the most common step used by the majority of martial arts students. We have seen this in the dojo, in tournaments, and so forth. In our definition, this is a risky distance. It is not wrong, it's just technically a risky defensive move. Why? Each time you move back, you are still exposing your body. It gives both you and your attacker an opportunity to hit or counter hit. It is basically just a glorified version of critical distance where two out of three times you will be hit.

You also need room to step back. This move can become a habit, and most of the time there is no room to move back. By stepping back with a front stance, you will have to absorb the force coming at you. It takes a high level of skill to be able to absorb that force without endangering yourself. Without a front stance, you need an outstanding balancing act to not be overbalanced (knocked over) and, if you don't fall, you will be driven back. In the dojo or tournaments, we see defenders going out of the ring when being pressed by multiple attacks. In other cases, they take one step back and just stand there, thinking they have outsmarted their opponents by changing range. Then they are surprised when their opponents step forward and hit them. Other times people just start backpedaling to avoid the incoming hits. They try to run backwards faster than their opponents can run forward. This goes on until the referee stops the fight.

In a real situation, there are no judges, no rules, and no rings. Most of the time, there is no room to back up.

There are many more effective directions you can take to move into defensive distance other than straight backward. You should spend considerable time practicing moving in these other directions. Even subtly moving to another direction (5 o'clock or 7 o'clock) has better strategic results than moving straight back.

Controlling defensive distance is a critical component in establishing what we call "control presence." Often someone trying to sneak into critical or offensive distance is the precursor to an attack. It doesn't matter how intimidating you think you are being. If an attacker can move into offensive or critical distance without you noticing, then he will be encouraged to attack.

DEFENSIVE DISTANCE

Step to an angle and block.

Safe Positioning

Safe distance is the core of placement, putting yourself where you can easily hit or counter your opponent while making it difficult for him to strike you.

By moving forward to 11 o'clock, you will put yourself closer to your opponent while his momentum will put him facing your former 6 o'clock. He has to change direction to hit you or block your counterattack, while you have an excellent position and placement. Your next move is an attack, while his is to re-orient to attack.

Realize that once you have this upper hand, you are not going to give it up. Not only can you attack, but you can counter his attempt to put you back into critical distance.

SAFE DISTANCE

Step into safe distance while blocking.

SAFE DISTANCE (continued)

Move into safe distance.

Strike without being struck.

Offensive Positioning

Offensive distance is moving to 1 o'clock with the intent to attack first. You attack the person when you recognize from his body language that he will attempt to hurt you.

By moving forward to 1 o'clock, you position yourself closer to your opponent, and your opponent is close to you, but not directly facing you. You must flip the ON switch, you must attack like your life depends on the move. You must plan and practice this tirelessly. When you move to this position there should be no half measures or hesitation.

Once you are familiar with these positions, someone trying to slide into attack position will be blatantly obvious—as will

OFFENSIVE DISTANCE

Step to 1 o'clock and attack.

his intention. By calmly manipulating defensive distance to counter his attempts to move into attack distance, you establish control presence. You tell him you are in control and that you are not safe to attack, because you know what he is up to. If you do decide to let it happen, you are also controlling where he will be allowed to attack. You just let him slip into what he thinks is a good attack position (which in simpler terms is called a trap).

Posture

Posture is defined as how you hold your body. It is when the body is put into motion where posture really puts the pedal to the metal.

Let's look at blocking as a way to explain this concept. What most people think of as blocks are in fact postures. They are the end result of moving into that posture (body position). However, they are not the block itself. The block happens by flowing into that posture. The posture is where the movement stops. It does not go beyond that point because by the time that posture is achieved, the block is already done. Having said that, now that the job is done, you can easily flow into another move.

That posture is a reference point in a flow of movement. Do not think of separate movements that end in a posture. Think of a single, flowing movement that passes through these postures, like a river runs past different towns. The river doesn't stop flowing.

This small shift in perspective will have a major effect on how you look at blocking specifically and movement overall.

There are many elements involved in good posture; it is never about just one thing. Often these elements seem paradoxical. In truth, because they are so all-encompassing, they become flexible. They are offensive and defensive, strategic and tactical, and the definition and creation of options. They allow delivery of power, ability to receive your opponent's power, and much more.

By realizing that posture is never about just one thing, the previous statements begin to make sense. Proper posture accomplishes all kinds of things at once. It both protects you and prepares you for your next move. Improper posture may accomplish one thing—or it may not—but it will not address multiple issues.

In no other area is the need for error detection so pressing as in the subject of posture. Incorrect body posture is the source of many problems that plague you on the path to learning martial arts. This task is made much more complicated by the fact that many paper masters don't fully understand posture themselves. The postures they teach do not meet the criteria of multiple purposes. Consequently, the explanations they give about application and execution of the moves tend to be shallow and one-dimensional.

Worse, the techniques themselves don't work as advertised because important components are missing. Either the teacher was never taught, wasn't around long enough to learn, or just didn't bother to learn these components. You cannot teach what you do not know.

Proper posture is a flowing, living process. It is not robotic. It flows into achieving the placement; it is not the end unto itself. Flowing from one posture to another is like a river. Breaking this up and stopping in different postures is like damming that river. If any legitimate complaint can be leveled against the way that many hard-style martial arts are practiced, it is that most have turned their postures into dams that stop the river's flow. Postures are not dams, they are towns the river flows through.

You can use the idea of posture to check if you are leaving yourself exposed to counterattack. Throughout this book, you will see photos that show different ways to do moves. Comparing the two postures, you will see one person is exposed to counterattack at various times during the move, while the other is constantly covered.

The proper posture gives you many important advantages: structure, base, stability, ease of motion, control of centerline, an ingrained defensive screen, and open pathways to launch offenses, to name just a few. Improper posture gives you none of these and leaves you vulnerable.

Structure is your body's ability to deal with delivering or receiving force. The foundation of structure is your skeleton. Your bones are the means to deliver force, but they also are how you resist the effects of gravity. Disrupting a person's structure is a fundamental for throws and takedowns.

Proper posture utilizes your body's natural structure. There are certain positions that are the most structurally sound and where you are able to handle force without moving or collapsing. Your martial art posture should put you in your body's strongest positions.

Much of the time the source of the flaws in such postures can be traced to the fact that people have been conditioned to punch to meet the objectives of contemporary point sparring, in which the primary thing needed to score is speed. The objective is to merely hit the opponent before he can hit you. This holds true for a punch or a kick. How often in point contests do you see people kicking or punching at the same time, hoping to be the first to land?

Many practitioners have sacrificed proper structure that could deliver the force of one's blows for light flicks that have nothing behind them but the weight of the fist and whatever glove they happen to be wearing. A fly may score a point for hitting an elephant, but even at top speed, the elephant simply won't notice.

This isn't to say that speed isn't important, only that speed is one component among many needed if you want to defend yourself. Many people who overemphasize speed are trying to (1) compensate for a lack of structure, (2) make up for lost time after pausing or stopping their movement, or (3) make up for lost time after putting in extra, unnecessary, and time-wasting movements. Unfortunately, the result of this extra speed is usually sloppier—and structurally more unsound—techniques.

They may well be fast, and while that will be an asset in meeting the objectives of point sparring, it will not necessarily translate into an advantage for the transmission of power or the objectives of self-defense. The key is to become faster while maintaining proper structure. Speed is one asset among many that you should invest in. Putting all your stock in speed is very risky if your objective is anything but beating someone to the punch just to score a point. If you sacrifice proper structural integrity for speed alone, your punches may be dangerous, but they are just as likely to injure you as your opponent.

If you aren't holding proper alignment of your wrist, elbow, or shoulder, the force you are trying to transmit into your opponent will drive back into you through these errors. Usually your punching arm will just bend, but you can jam your arm or worse. It is your structure that not only helps you deliver force, but enables you to withstand the impact without crumbling or being injured.

Proper posture gives you another important element: *base*. When we use the idea of base we mean it in two ways. First, it is the foundation your structure is built on. It is your connection to the earth that allows stability, but it also allows movement. The second meaning of base is in a military sense, like a fire base. It is a staging area from which you can launch sorties. But it also is mobile. It is not rooted in one location, like a permanent military base here in the United States. It is a fire base that can move to meet the changing needs of the situation. Proper posture gives you both definitions.

You can check for proper structure and base in your posture by simply having someone walk into you. Have that person put his chest against your limb and walk toward you. If your limb collapses or you are knocked over, then something is wrong with the posture. You can check your stances this way, too.

Stability is the combined result of structure and base. It allows you to deal with and generate force, whether standing or moving. It is the ability to handle force through moving base that keeps your structure from being disrupted. More importantly, it allows you to keep everything within your control. In doing so, you can direct all your movement where you want it to go (placement). Everything is moving in one tight, concise package, instead of flying off in other directions or wobbling. A proper posture gives you this stability by combining structure and base to achieve your ends.

Another thing that the proper posture gives you is ease of motion from one posture to another. These predetermined postures are closely related to one another. It is a small matter of weight transfer to flow from one to another.

Proper posture also gives you *control of centerline*. Controlling centerline is a critical strategic element. Although it is possible to win without controlling centerline, not controlling it exponentially increases the difficulty of winning. You can do it, but expect to work at least four times harder.

To understand centerline, imagine a pole running through your body from the top of your head into the ground. This is your vertical axis. This is the imaginary line around which your body pivots. It is the center of your mass on a vertical axis. Now imagine the same in your opponent.

Centerline is the shortest distance between those two points and is the connection between them. Here is where our definition varies from that of most martial artists. If you were to look at this from overhead, it would look like a thin line. Indeed, centerline is very thin. However, if you look at it from a side view, imagine it to be a sheet of glass. It is not thick, but it is wide and tall. This is the area you must control, both high and low. Your posture must put you into a body position where you can use both hands and feet to control centerline.

You will find that many errors that have crept into modern martial arts postures are based on failing to place some part of yourself to control centerline. This leaves you open and vulnerable to attacks in much of the same way an open window in a high-crime area invites burglary.

Take a look at the comparison photos we use throughout this book. Often what you will see is one person covering centerline while the other unwittingly exposes it. In time, you will begin to see this failure to control centerline at a glance, whether in a photograph or a student.

Perhaps one of the most misunderstood concepts in modern martial arts is the idea of a *defensive screen*. This largely results from a decay in understanding the multifaceted benefits of correct posture. Think of a window with thousands of flies outside. As long as the window stays closed, no flies get in. Unfortunately, it is necessary to open the window now and then. When that happens, flies get in.

A major source of errors in the martial arts arises from the attempts of people to keep the flies out. Some people, through poor posture, leave the window open all the time and wonder why flies come and go at will. Others attempt to solve the problem by speed. They zip from posture to posture. This would be like trying to open and close the window in the shortest time possible. Still others try to solve the problem with a combination of speed and obstructions. These obstructions can be excessive hits or fast blocks. This is like trying to open and close the window quickly while shooing flies away at the same time.

The problem with any of these ideas is that the window is still wide open without any real barrier to keep flies out. This is what happens with incorrect postures; the windows are left open (holes) and the flies (attacks) get in. This is especially true when you move. Most people don't realize that in moving from posture to posture, they should not be exposed. Or maybe they do realize it and just can't cover it. If an incorrect posture is an open window, moving from incorrect posture to incorrect posture is an open door. That is where a majority of flies get in.

A correct posture is like putting a screen in front of that window. This is what we mean by a defensive screen—the flies (attacks) are checked in their attempts to get in. By controlling centerline, you are taking a major step toward establishing a constant defensive screen. In a posture, that window should be closed. Even though the window is open when you move from one posture to another, the movement from these two points creates a screen. Again, let us state, it is not the posture that is the

Ready.

Transfer weight, cover centerline.

Step, drop elbow, transfer weight, block.

block, it is moving into that posture. Because the posture has these defensive screen capabilities, those capabilities are extended to the act of moving into it. It is not speed; it is putting something in front of an opening to keep attacks from getting through.

A point that we will address later regarding the strategic use of defensive screens is this: If the screen isn't there, it is a trap. We want you to come in through that "hole."

The final point regarding correct posture is that it automatically gives you *pathways* to launch offensives. Like the military fire base, it is a staging area for those attacks. You do not need to cock back or in any other way prepare to make an attack more powerful. Your structure, base, and stability are already there waiting for deployment. All you have to do is move into position and fire.

Placement

Placement is the total objective of a technique. Good placement should be everyone's goal. Why? Placement is the culmination of everything we have discussed coming together in one, overwhelming combination. Weight transfer, position, and posture all come together to explode into your opponent.

What is placement? It is just that—placing your hands, feet, and body (posture) in such a manner that your position is to your advantage. This position should also place your attacker at a disadvantage for his next move and control his intent to finish his technique. You should have the upper hand and, at the very least, control of what your attacker might do next. To be able to accomplish this, simple movements are required, but hands, feet, and body movements should be synchronized and in harmony.

Let's illustrate the basic movements. For the purpose of imagining the fight scenario, we will put the attacker at 12 o'clock. Putting the attacker at this position is how we teach our students and will be used throughout the book as an example.

> **Hands**—As your attacker lunges and strikes with his right hand, your response would be deflecting/blocking with your left hand. Let's assume he attacks you with a straight punch. You block with a middle level, inside-outside, "reverse" block (uchi uke).
>
> **Feet**—At the same time you step to 11 o'clock with a smooth weight transfer. As you step, your weight moves forward while you deflect the strike.
>
> **Body**—As you do the weight transfer, your body will want to move toward 11 o'clock, but you must resist the

urge by maintaining or redirecting your body motion and your eyes to 12 o'clock.

After you have executed all these integral parts, you will feel the benefit of placement. The advantages are:

1. By going to 11 o'clock, you are moving away from the line of fire. This is safe distance.
2. Your hands and body will be close to your attacker, but it would take a much longer reach for your attacker, and he must adjust his position to continue.
3. Your deflection or blocking technique will disturb the attacker's forward motion. The harder or faster his forward motion, the more angle he travels from 6 o'clock to 5, 4, or 3 o'clock. The more angles he has to take, the more advantages you have.
4. Your attacker's kick is either immobilized, rendered inactive, or becomes useless. Immobilized means that he has to change directions to kick, while your position allows instant response.
5. Placement will give you an advantage in executing sweeps.
6. Last but not least, placement of your hand on his arm, slightly above his elbow, will prevent or slow his next response. By jamming his arm, you keep him from moving his shoulder. As long as his right shoulder is not moving, his left arm is useless for a forward strike. He may attempt to do a back fist with his left hand, but he has to spin around blindly. The advantage for you is your hands are already in front of you, and it will take only a slight motion to block the incoming back fist.

~ 3 ~

Blocking

While most people have the right intention when it comes to blocking, their execution is insufficient to meet the goal of the technique. What is that specific goal? Not to get hit!

Burn this simple concept into your consciousness. Put it above everything else and dispose of anything that interferes with it. It is not failure to meet that goal that has caused such confusion about blocking. It is losing that focus in a flood of details that is both the problem and the reason why it is so hard to fix.

Not getting hit is the first and last word on blocking; everything else is details. Details have a habit, however, of taking over a process, almost to the point where they become primary and achieving the goal becomes secondary. The fuss over finding a better way to block has eclipsed the goal of "don't get hit." Lip service is still paid to the idea. But for all the arguing over the "right" way to block, martial arts students sure get hit a lot.

So what should you be looking at instead of details? Here are a few fundamentals.

Fundamentals of Blocking

Blocking is a technique directed at a certain target to arrest or deflect an opponent's attack. The flow of action is multidirectional: up, down, or side to side. The power and speed of blocks or deflections vary depending on the objective—stopping further attack by changing the direction of this strike and controlling the next action, or counterattacking to discourage further hits. The traditional way of blocking to stop something requires using a force greater than that which set the object in motion. This is not necessary to have an effective block. Your objective is to change the velocity or direction of the strikes.

It is difficult to block powerfully until you first learn to do it correctly. You should wait until you have developed consistency in applying basic movements before you attempt to develop power in the techniques. Also, you should not worry about speed at this time. Practice the basics correctly, otherwise you are likely to develop fast, sloppy, ineffective techniques.

At this phase, you will have more speed and power than ever before—not as a result of body strength, but because of refinement of your technique. Your goal now is to appear to be moving effortlessly.

There are many different blocking techniques to learn. But, we must first analyze the movements by imagining how people will react in attacking or defending in actual fights or combat. Study the basic principles of the techniques diligently. Contrary to the popular belief that to execute effective blocks and strikes we must utilize power, an effective move does not depend on power alone. When there is no feeling of power or resistance, the blows and the strikes are effective.

Blocking

Imagine good tennis players in action, how relaxed their body movements are. They trust their rackets to do the work. They are relaxed, not rigid, but natural. They concentrate their power on the spot where they will hit the ball with the racket. They do not have to hold their rackets very tightly before they hit the ball. As a matter of fact, they hold their rackets rather loosely. It is the same in martial arts. If you are holding your fist tightly before applying the technique, you will feel the tension. That tension will slow the speed or delay your execution. Be natural.

Sound difficult? Not if you start focusing on the fundamentals of blocking instead of the details, and we are going to separate the two now.

Blocking is where the rubber meets the road in the fighting business. If attacks are regularly getting through, something is wrong, usually in one of three places: (1) the type of block being used, (2) what is being taught as blocking, or (3) how the block is being taught. This can be summed up: (1) wrong move, and (2) parts missing.

Widespread adaptation of blocks has been developed by so-called masters. The variations are often as detrimental as they are complementary to blocking. In fact, the subject of blocking gets rather complex. These days it is not uncommon for there to be a division between how you block in sports, kata, and self-defense. The student is trained in as many as three radically different systems in the same martial art! This can create some definite dilemmas, especially when people run around and try to solve the problems with the same thinking that created them.

Unfortunately by creating such complicated "solutions," students are not trained effectively in any of them. This results in students knowing how to handle simple tasks in a safe environment or a dojo situation. In the long run however, their dojo knowledge will not be applicable in a real fighting situation. This is why we insist on returning to the fundamental goal of don't get hit.

The same can be said about blocking—either you are getting hit or you aren't. This is why we must evaluate the objective of blocks, even if it seems almost insultingly remedial. You have to identify the goal and let that define your actions. Defining a goal compels you to decide what you are trying to accomplish. It gives you standards to which you can compare your actions or solutions to determine their success. Otherwise, you will get lost in the details.

If you are getting hit on a regular basis, don't just shrug it off as part of the martial art or sparring process. Something is wrong. It's time to go back to the fundamentals and reexamine what you think you know about blocking.

Importance of Posture, Placement, and Positioning

Blocking consists of two main elements that combine to create a greater whole. They are creating structure (posture) and moving into position. Together they create a third element, placement.

Any block must meet these standards to be continuously effective. If it doesn't, that is why you get hit. This simple formula defines a major problem with what are taught as both "traditional" and "improved" blocks. You're getting hit because (a) your structure is weak, (b) it's not in the right place, (c) you're just standing there, or (d) any combination of the above.

Boiling it down to its most basic component, blocking is a matter of putting something that can handle incoming force in the right place to intercept it, while at the same time moving the target out of the way. Everything else is details.

Now that we have defined what must be present, we can look at blocking in an entirely different and more practical light. We have a standard against which to compare what we are doing. With this standard, we can also begin to see why so many blocks fail. Don't be fooled by the fact that your instructor can block in this manner and you can't. If something is being patched with either muscle or speed, then it will only work for the instructor, and it will only work for him against students or lesser trained, slower opponents. Remember, a block must work consistently before you can call it effective. If something is effective, it works across the board. That means you should be able to do it, too, and against all kinds of attacks.

With this in mind, let's start looking at some of the factors you will face and why such simple answers of posture, position, and placement work when more complicated ones don't.

To begin with, we must recognize the difference between light, fast, sport contact and punches that are intended to hurt you. There is a big difference. In the point-oriented ring, delivery of power is not an issue. Speed is paramount. Fast, light punches are the norm. They streak in, tag you, and give your opponents points. They don't have to hurt, they just have to touch. A myth that arises from this is that all someone would have to do is "crank up the power" to make this kind of blow a knockout strike. Not true: it is fast because it lacks the very elements that could deliver power.

In light of this trend toward light, quick hits, it is obvious that blocks had to change to adapt to these circumstances. Traditional blocking techniques would be inadequate against someone who is trained in boxing or is a smart street fighter. Fighting a boxer face to face could be the first (and possibly last) mistake a martial arts student makes. If he has never been taught how to block a jab, if he has never learned to move on the angle—he probably will not fare well against a trained boxer. Often, just to make matters worse, students have learned from one-step sparring to move only straight backward or forward.

The other side of the coin is that light, fast blocks that work against quicker, insubstantial ring punches fail against the harder, more committed blows of someone who is trying to cause you serious damage. Notice that even in the ring, these kinds of blocks often fail when someone turns up the power. Still the lighter, faster blows are what most ring sparring martial artists are trained to block. Which demands that we ask: How could we expect them to react differently in a real fight?

Students must acknowledge the existence of and be prepared to fight not only karate or Tae Kwon Do players, but students using other martial arts techniques. They also must be armed against various types of street-fighting maneuvers. This means students must learn to defend themselves against attacks from all levels and against jabs, punches, kicks, or sweeps while they are in motion. Now if that sounds like an impossible task, it is—at least from the standpoint of how most people teach blocking (sparring, kata, self-defense).

Coming back to the idea of posture, position, and placement, the task is more manageable. You realize the task at hand is not to learn ten thousand blocks to handle each and every type of attack and correctly choose the right block on the fly while being attacked. The task is learning how to combine these three elements to handle whatever kind of attack you are facing. Instead of developing a new way to block for every different kind of attack, work at learning posture, position, and placement and how to apply them in all your blocking.

Teaching these ideas is a process, not a one-step event. There is no one drill that, like a computer program CD, installs everything at once. Throughout this chapter, ideas that must be emphasized will be pointed out to help you develop drills, find useful training tips, and identify common problems.

One must carefully consider the influence of patching and ring sparring in both kata and self-defense training, especially when it comes to blocking. Unfortunately, when trying to solve one problem, another is created. Quite often preparatory moves, such as "chambering" (the unnecessary cocking back to throw a punch that people believe will increase speed and power) have been added into "traditional" katas. This allows for creation of speed to assist in the block. While true that these moves allow the average person to block harder through acceleration, there are unintended consequences. Chambering moves not only take longer to execute, but they leave the blocker exposed.

As an example, if you are doing a middle knife-hand block, there are styles that teach students to place their hands behind them and then accelerate them across their bodies into blocking position. This leaves your side fully exposed and unprotected for at least a second—while you are out gathering speed to block harder.

Often this kind of movement has been justified as "fighting multiple attackers." But honestly, how realistic is that? How is the posture you take in these kinds of movement supposed to stop a blow? What kind of blow? Have you ever tried it? And to block without even looking? Do you really expect a second attacker to attack only once? To politely stand there and wait while you finish off his friend before attacking again? Come on now, a little healthy skepticism is in order here.

<u>MIDDLE KNIFE–HAND BLOCK</u>

Incorrect.

Incorrect.

In light of these questions, the only logical explanation for this kind of extra action is chambering for more acceleration.

Let's return to the fundamental of blocking: don't get hit. If this is your goal, any action not consistent with it must be dropped. Chambering to block is not consistent with the avowed goal. Look at what it does: it goes out, comes back to the starting point, and then heads out to where the block needs to be. Even if it is moving faster on the way back, you are now covering three times the distance. This is on top of having wasted time chambering. This is supposed to work as a block? If this extra motion doesn't triple, it will at least double the time of execution. This is time you don't have to waste when a blow is already coming at you from the right range.

Now compare that with bringing only one hand to the side of your face while leaving your elbow pointed at your opponent. Then dropping the elbow: this is not only faster, but also more structurally sound. It gives you the power you need to block in a very short space, all the while leaving your other hand out to protect yourself (defensive screen).

This brings up the second criteria for meeting your goal of not being hit. Leave something else out there to protect yourself while blocking or preparing to block. Quite often, people winding up for a block leave a pathway open for a blow. Leave either your other hand or the elbow of your blocking arm in front of you, but behind your block, to serve as a second line of defense if things go wrong.

You will find that this fundamental failure in posture is one of the more common reasons that blows get in. There is no defensive screen left in place when blocking. That means your block has no backup, nor do your punches, in case of a counterattack.

MIDDLE KNIFE–HAND BLOCK, FROM SIDE

Correct.

Correct.

In certain styles, someone tried to address this idea by teaching students to block on centerline. That is to say, the block actually stops on centerline. This is not what we are talking about. Blocking like this leaves half of your body exposed (especially if you don't move from that position). While centerline must be covered, your blocks need to cross centerline and move far enough to pass the incoming attack away from your body—not into it. You do this by either moving your body out of the way while blocking to your former centerline or blocking in a way that effectively covers that half of your body—out to your shoulder. In either case, you leave something else covering centerline as backup.

These two concepts of dropping extra movement and covering yourself aren't even the foundation of blocking, they are the ground that a foundation stands on. Without them, you can't even begin to build a foundation, much less a block. Unfortunately, many modern versions of supposedly traditional katas fail to create postures that generate these two foundations. With this screwy interpretation of kata, there is little wonder that one must make a distinction between kata, self-defense, and sparring.

If kata doesn't teach you how to defend yourself, why do it?

If your katas aren't assisting you to ingrain these two concepts, there is something wrong with the postures. Flip through books on your martial arts style and imagine how you would attack someone in the postures you see there. Do those postures meet the basic criteria of no extra movement and always covering yourself? Unfortunately, many students will accept a fictitious assertion made reasonably, yet forcefully by an instructor, even if it flies in the face of everything they know and experience—and even when the facts are in plain sight.

While we are talking basic groundwork, let's look at range. Eventually the student learns that he can never simply wait for an opponent to attack. He must be prepared and ready to react instantly to defend or, if necessary, attack. The window of opportunity is not open for long, and a student should take advantage when he sees it. Prepare and act.

But for a student to learn this, he or she must have a basic understanding of range. The student needs to realize that the attack really begins when the opponent moves into range. That is when you start controlling the situation, not when a blow is already streaking at your face. When that fundamental is grasped, then the idea we expressed in the last paragraph becomes less mystical and easier to understand, as does blocking in general.

Understanding range has another important aspect. If the attacker's punch doesn't reach you, there is no need to block. Feints lose much of their terror and effectiveness when you understand range. By knowing range, you realize it isn't a real attack from way over there, so you won't overreact and expose yourself to the real attack.

Students need to be able to recognize their range, their opponent's range, and safe distance. This is done by introducing the student to these fundamental issues before teaching blocking. Specific drills can be created to show reach, distance, and range of an opponent.

Stand back and throw a punch from out of range. Move forward, step by step, until the student learns at what range a hand or leg technique can strike. That is when it is time to block. By doing this, a student begins to understand the range of the attack and exact technique needed to achieve the objective of blocking. Understanding range is a prerequisite to learning positioning and placement.

Learning positioning and placement is critical to successfully executing an effective block. By combining these basic movements (i.e., block/deflect and stepping to the left, right, back, and forward), you can easily avoid the collision from the attacker's strikes or the force of the attacker's forward motion. This is deflection, which we will discuss later. Although deflection is a high level of blocking, let's stick with some more basic aspects because they are steps toward reaching deflection.

Let's take this opportunity to look at how range, posture, positioning, and placement can apply to blocking and at the same time allow you to check the effectiveness of what you are being trained in. In order to teach effective blocking, instructors should make sure that training partners do not throw "courtesy punches." It is common in many schools for partners to throw punches in training that intentionally fall short. This behavior, although seemingly benign and helpful, creates a host of misunderstandings about both blocking and range. It also fails to reveal problems with posture and hinders understanding of range, positioning, and timing for a block.

An incoming blow must be in range to connect. If it is not blocked, it will land. We are not saying that students need to try to drive each other's noses out the back of their skulls. They can punch slowly and still include mass, movement, and correct range. The object is to help your training partner develop the means to handle the force of an incoming blow. By feeling this, the student learns that being in the right place with a structure that can handle the incoming force is more important than just getting there quickly. The blocking student needs to recognize range and feel the incoming force to experiment with proper body posture and to find the proper position to handle the incoming force.

Remember in the last chapter when we spoke of testing the structural integrity of postures by walking into them? The same idea applies here. By insisting that students not throw courtesy punches, they not only learn what force feels like, but the effects it has on their structure and the problems that occur from bad posture. Without this feedback, it is difficult to learn the nuances of blocking, much less make sure the critical components are present when actually trying to avoid getting hit.

With this in mind, students should first concentrate on the big features of a block: the gross body and limb movement. They should learn to focus on executing the technique slowly and with large movements. Special focus needs to be given to putting a good body structure in the correct place. It is easier for students to see these ideas manifest in larger, basic moves. That is why they must start big and work toward smaller movement. Later on, as their skill becomes more refined, they can start to emphasize the smaller details of the movements: speed, timing, application of the techniques, and so forth.

A training aid is having students practice in front of a mirror. They must, however, have a specific focus when doing this. Many students when looking in the mirror focus on their hands and arms alone. This is incorrect. The student needs to specifically be looking at his or her body and watching how the block or forearm passes before it, covering it. This small, but important shift in perspective allows the student to analyze the effectiveness of what he is doing. If parts of his body are left exposed during the motion, they are "windows" an attack can come through. These holes or windows usually result from improper posture and sloppy movement from posture to posture. Using a mirror in this manner assists the student to learn proper posture and movement faster and easier.

What you don't want students to do is speed through the blocks. If a person's posture leaves open windows, is it not feasible that he would try to close them through speed and power?

Blocking

How do most people attempt to create speed and power? By winding up and chambering. We're back to that, again. Unfortunately, this opens more windows. By moving slowly through blocks, the mirror shows you these holes and errors.

Perhaps the most important criteria for blocking is your elbow position. It should not be far away from your body nor overly out from the side of your rib. Make it a habit to drop the elbow straight down after the block to protect or to close the opening in the front of your body.

The elbow needs to be near your body for many reasons: proper focus, coverage, avoidance of overshooting your posture to proper structure. Let's look at them one at a time.

Many people, when they think of a block, focus on their hands and wrists. In fact, their hands tend to move first, with their elbows simply dragged along in the process. This is what we mean when we say "sloppy movement" from posture to posture.

One of the biggest problems with this is that it just shoots your hand into space. Yes, it is faster. The problem is it is very easy to overshoot your mark when moving that fast. With your hand wobbling out there, there is no sense of spatial relationship with your body. If you think about it, this is rather silly. That block is supposed to be protecting you. What is it doing somewhere way over yonder? How is it going to keep you from getting hit if you don't know where it is?

Then there is the problem of chambering movement that we discussed earlier. The extra movement makes it even harder to find the correct position when you are blocking from the hands.

Focusing on your hands, swing your arm from one extreme to another. Reach over one shoulder as far as you can and swing your arm horizontally to the other extreme. Now estimate the circumference you have covered. We can cover a distance of

<u>GENERIC BLOCK</u>

Ready stance.

Cover centerline and shift weight.

Block with body movement.

about eight feet by swinging our arms. In that entire distance, a student is supposed to find an exact spot halfway through the arc to stop his hand for the block and at top speed? Good luck.

By focusing on putting your elbow in the correct position, however, your hand will, by extension, move into the correct place. You will find that advanced practitioners of an art have unconsciously learned to bring their focus inward to other parts of their bodies. Help students by telling them about this focal point up front, instead of letting them struggle to develop this unconscious awareness.

An example of this incorrect focus while blocking can be found in the down block. Many people chamber before blocking this way. This leaves them vulnerable if the original attack is a feint or if it wasn't heading where they thought it was going. Even though they are moving their hand very fast, no protection is going to be there until the very end of the movement. Unfortunately, with the extra distance and time it takes to wind up, the block probably will arrive too late.

It's far simpler and faster to just drop the elbow to cover the ribs and then drop your arm. Even if the blow goes somewhere else, you are covered along your side. You don't need to chamber to hit harder. If your elbow is in the right place, you will have more than sufficient force to get the job done. By dropping your elbow for the block, you also create an alignment of the arm that adds power. Any body motion you perform will be transmitted through the elbow that is resting against your side.

This in contrast to the extra gyrations and movement that people try to stick in to compensate for a lack of training in the fundamentals (one, two, three, . . . nine, ten).

If your elbow is in the wrong place, you lose power. The connection to your body movement is lost and, by extension, so is structure. This allows powerful blows to blast through. To regain enough power to keep an attack from plowing through, you have to overcompensate. You now must engage more of the upper body than just the biceps when trying to fling the hand into position. Or you can take the more common route and wind up to block harder.

If you overly focus on your hand as the source of your block, there is a very good chance you will overshoot the optimum location. This commonly results in reopening yourself to attack. By overshooting, your other side is exposed because you cannot return fast enough to protect it from another attack. If you focus on keeping your elbow guarding your side, however, it is difficult to overshoot in this manner. While it is obvious as to which is the "correct" block, ask yourself how many times you see the incorrect version in sparring.

By focusing on your hands instead of your elbow, it is too easy to lose proper posture. From there it is a small step to trying to fix the problem with speed. To add insult to injury, by focusing on your fist or forearm, your hand will probably hit the attacker's shin, creating a lot of pain and setting up a much riskier scenario. Believing your hands are the source of your block, you also are more likely to reach for an incoming hit.

You don't have to reach for a strike—like death and taxes, it is certain the attack is coming to you. If you focus on your elbow, you will begin to develop an instinctive understanding of defensive range. If an attack is not in range, you don't have to block at all. On the other hand, if you focus on your hand, you will tend to overextend your block to meet the incoming attack, even if it would have fallen short.

This also happens when people attempt to "hit" with their blocks, a matter we will discuss later.

Blocking

FLAWED DOWN BLOCK

Incorrect: ready.

Incorrect: wind up.

Incorrect: elbows out and overcompensating.

PROPER DOWN BLOCK

Ready stance.

*Correct: transfer weight,
cover centerline.*

Correct: elbow drops with step.

*Correct: hand drops with
weight transfer.*

If the elbow is in the wrong place, you also lose "timing" by trying to race with your hand against the incoming blow. Everything that we have discussed thus far is rolled into this last point. If you are focusing on your hands to get there fast and hard enough to block, you must shoot them out at high speed. Going this fast, stopping that far out in space in just the right position, and doing it all in time to deflect an incoming blow is very difficult. Then it becomes all about timing. If you aren't in exactly the right place at exactly the right time, the blow will get through. This is what we mean by racing a blow, and it is why people so often lose this contest.

If your elbow is in the correct place, your hand will simply fall into position to intercept the blow. Your block is no longer dependent on timing, but rather moving into the correct posture and position. In this manner, your block rolls out from your body. With your elbow in place, your block is heading down the highway for a head-on collision with the incoming attack. Think about it: your elbow is already there, so the incoming blow is going to be intercepted. It's not a matter of "if" they will crash, but "when." This makes timing much less important.

Your elbow in the correct location gives your posture structure to handle that crash. Your opponent's attack may be a speeding car, but what is coming toward him is a train.

Myths of Blocking

Until now, we have largely addressed problems that arise from poor posture. Blocking, however, is a two-part process: posture and position. It is moving into position that gives you critical placement. Movement is the lost "art" of blocking. To explain the importance, we're going to talk about it in terms of common myths about blocking.

MYTH: "I'M ONLY GOING TO BE ATTACKED ONCE."

Often we hear the myth that the attacker will only have time to attack once before you retaliate with a devastating counterpunch that will drop him. Welcome to fantasy—reality will hurt a whole lot more.

This single attack idea is not only an assumption; it becomes ingrained in the hearts and minds of many martial arts students. Like the idea of lip service paid to not getting hit, a large number of martial arts schools talk about handling multiple attacks, but they train their students in a one-attack mindset. Then these students get hit with the second, third, and fourth blows.

REALITY: YOU WILL BE ATTACKED MULTIPLE TIMES.

Unless you are attacked by a drunken man who has a hard time standing upright, expect to have to deal with multiple attacks from the same opponent. You will be attacked by a barrage of punches and kicks or both, so you must be prepared accordingly.

Unfortunately, much of the training in martial arts schools does not prepare you for handling this reality. Multiple attacks are a strategic reality with which you must deal. The way most people block is a tactical response. It might stop one attack, but it does nothing to address the bigger strategic problems. Blocking must be strategic, not just tactical. An important aspect of this book is getting this message across to students and teachers alike. Sadly though, we also understand that many schools will not understand or heed this critical message.

There is a tendency to attack and then back off. One reason is that students drill in one-step fighting, over and over, without explanations. One-step is a good basic for eventual free fighting; however, most students never really move on. We see many black belts competing in point fighting and still using one-step attitudes: "Let me hit you, and I hope the judges see it and stop the fight." This assumption is seen all over the world. Students are mired in one-step sparring (ippon kumite). Although this basic practice is very important, in reality, it will not work unless the attacker is behaving like a drunk who expects one blow to work. An additional problem this creates is it often encourages the defender not to move. Why should he worry about moving off line if he is only going to be attacked once?

SOLUTION: DON'T LEAVE YOURSELF OPEN TO THE ORIGINAL ATTACK OR ANY FOLLOWING ATTACKS.

This is easier said than done, but it can be accomplished with proper movement. Practice of the fundamentals of posture, position, and placement is critical. Understanding the attacker's intention and what to do about it is vital to comprehending blocking techniques. Taking advantage of your hand and body movement will enhance blocking effectiveness.

Many people who are trained to move off line do not do so in a strategic manner. They are so busy getting out of the way that they fail to move into proper position to counterattack. Without proper position they cannot create placement. Before they can counterattack they must move into position. The bad news is that while they are moving into attack position so too is their opponent. Moving into correct position in the first place solves this problem.

While watching a boxing match we were very impressed with the boxers' use of hands, distance, and circular movement. Moving away from the target is always the objective. The boxers always had their faces and bodies protected either with their hands or by moving away.

Moving from the straight line (firing line) is a must. You must learn to move into safe, offensive, and defensive distance. Practice this often. Movement, combined with blocking, controls where an opponent can attack you. It doesn't matter if he is launching another attack; you've moved. His second attack is going to the wrong place, and your block is making it hard for him to follow you.

A block alone is never as effective as a block combined with movement. Always move away from where you are blocking. Attempting to block without moving is an invitation to be hit, not only by the first blow, but the next one. This is why you must understand safe and offensive distance; strategic movement is as much a part of blocking as your elbows and hands.

Knowing where your opponent is attempting to strike sets up your defense. Lure him to the spots you want him to attack, then you are prepared to guard, deflect, and counter. A critical part of defending yourself is to use parts of your body to dictate the area where your opponent will attack. This is either one of the most crucial parts of learning martial arts or one of the most neglected. Any place where there is no defensive screen is a trap.

MYTH: ONE BLOCK IS ALL YOU NEED.

In essence, this is a true statement. But to achieve this objective, you must go through years of training and practicing basic fundamentals and applications. You must master timing, judging distance and utilizing technique to your advantage. You must be able to deflect and instantly take advantage of the situation with some kind of move to stall or take away the attacker's momentum. Many instructors do not know how to take advantage of the situation and will always go back to those techniques they are comfortable using.

This myth also arises from repeated one-step sparring. Consequently, minds and bodies will remember one thing—to respond to one strike with a deadly counterattack. While this sounds good in theory, the difference between theory and practice is in theory there is no difference. In practice, unless you do something more than just sticking your arm out to block, you are going to get hit.

REALITY: BY FAILING TO MOVE WHEN BLOCKING, PEOPLE MAKE IT INCREDIBLY EASY TO HIT THEM.

Consider this problem: Most people are so intent on getting a block out that not only are they not moving, they are not seeing what they are leaving exposed. In their haste, they aren't just encouraging another blow, they are helping it succeed.

If you do not move, your one-block tactic will fail against your opponent's multiple-blow strategy. Going back to the open window analogy, by not moving when they block, most people close one window while opening one right next to it.

There are several possibilities here. The first would be the same fly coming in through either of these windows. This happens when your block isn't in place in time and his blow still gets in. Or your block misses because its in the wrong place (bad posture). Both of these would have his attack coming through the first window. Or he punches again with the same hand after you have blocked. This would bring his second attack in behind your block (the other window). He is just as likely to hit with his other hand. This, too, would come in through the second window you opened. Pretty much any way you look at it, you are going to get hit.

Everything we have just said goes double when you attempt to "hit" with a block. It is common to go charging off into the boonies to get that extra force to knock away the blow. In doing so, you leave both windows wide open. This is especially true since most people root into position to create a base to strike from when they try to hit. This makes them sitting ducks for the next attack. They have rooted in critical distance, and their limbs are out past hell and gone.

SOLUTION: ONE BLOCK SETS UP THE FLOW TO ANOTHER.

Your elbows only need to flow mere inches from one pose to another. The bulk of the strategic work is being done by moving into position. By shifting your body, you have less need to move your elbow very far.

If the range is correct and a target is threatened, move the target. When you do, there is nothing for your opponent to hit. Not only has the window been moved, but the whole building is relocated. When you do this, your "block" becomes not only a deflection, but a check to keep your opponent from following you. You've moved and haven't left a forwarding address.

In truth, we're kind of hesitant to use the word "block." We would rather use the words "deflect" or "tap." Our objective is to always use very limited energy or movement in combination with deflection and avoidance in order not to get hit. Your block "covers" moving the windows. It serves as a rearguard action as you shift your windows out of range of your opponent's next planned attack. Once his plans are foiled by your movement, he must reformulate his strategy. This is time you can use to launch your offense.

This rearguard action also should keep you from trying to

reach for a block. You don't have to reach anywhere; all you have to do is block to where you have been.

MYTH: YOU HAVE TO BLOCK HARD AND FAST TO MAKE IT WORK.

This misconception has arisen because of a poor understanding of posture, as well as lack of body movement when blocking. The attitude is, "My blocks aren't working, so I must block harder and faster." This is analogous to saying, "We're in a hole, boys! We have to get out, so dig faster!" This patch of speed and muscle in blocking doesn't get you out of the problem, it just digs you deeper.

REALITY: REMEMBER THAT ADVANCEMENT IN THE MARTIAL ARTS IS
A MATTER OF SUBTLETY AND REFINEMENT.

You don't have to build a wall to stop an incoming attack. In fact, you don't really have to stop it at all. All you have to do is disrupt it to make it ineffective. We liken this to throwing a handful of pebbles in front of an annoying skateboarder. All of a sudden his control over those very things that were working for him (speed, momentum, and movement) start going horribly wrong. His problem is that while his control of these factors is gone, the aspects themselves are still affecting him. Like that skateboarder who suddenly and unexpectedly finds a pebble, he's going to be kind of busy trying to keep from falling.

Most attackers expect your face to stop their forward momentum. Not to be the bearer of bad tidings, but you are the opponent, and by definition, an opponent is *not* on your side. So don't help him beat you by standing there and trying to block hard enough to stop him. By standing and blocking hard, you might as well be saying, "Here, let me catch you and keep you from falling, so you can keep on beating me up."

SOLUTION: PROPER POSE AND MOVING INTO POSITION WILL WREAK HAVOC ON AN OPPONENT'S ATTACK AND HIS ABILITY TO HIT YOU AGAIN.

Most people do not attack correctly, that is, within range and with structure and balance. This makes them particularly vulnerable to deflection. The harder they attack, the worse it is when you are not there to catch them.

You, however, have to make sure that the pose you take in conjunction with moving into position creates this deflection. If the posture you take leaves windows open, that is where you will be hit next.

It is not that there are so many sneaky fighters out there who are good enough to find small cracks in your defense. It's that most people's defenses are wide open and are combined with a lack of movement. It isn't a matter of how does an attacker sneak in, it's more a choice of countless open holes that the defender has unwittingly left open.

While you can correct a great many of these problems by putting up defensive screens—putting your hand, knee, or forearm on centerline, adjusting your elbow position, repositioning your body, and so forth—consider which way you need to position yourself to move that screened window out of range.

You can help solve this problem by practicing in front of a mirror. Take a "blocking" pose and look to see what is left open and vulnerable to attack. An attack will come through those open windows. And if you stand still, that window is vulnerable to an attack crashing through, even if you screen it.

Now practice moving away from the block. Either use the line between mirror sections or place a long piece of tape vertically on the single pane. Start the move with the tape on centerline (in front of your nose). Imagine the blow is coming in from that line of tape. As you block, move your body, so your block is in line with the tape but your body is safely to the side. Your block should be between your body and the tape. That window is now out of reach.

Although this is a seemingly obvious exercise, do it repeatedly until blocking and moving in the correct direction are automatic reactions. Even experienced martial artists get confused at first; instead of moving away from the block, they will move into it. This will not deflect the incoming blow, but will suck it right into you. Do this drill using different types of blocks and from different angles. Stand in different positions as though the blows are coming at you from different directions. Don't try to apply the concept of position and posture in sparring until you can smoothly move away and block while doing this exercise.

Give yourself small, practical goals to work toward in this drill. See if you are blocking effectively, in combination with moving your body into position. Look to see if there are holes. Check to make sure your elbow is not moving more than ten inches to flow into another pose. If you have to move more than that, something is out of kilter with either your posture, your positioning, or your understanding of range.

You can use this exercise to refine many different aspects of blocking. When you get bored working on one aspect, focus on perfecting another. There are countless variations you can create. You are limited only by how deeply you want to understand blocking.

CONCLUSION: THE PURPOSE OF BLOCKING IS TO AVOID BEING HIT—
NOT TO DO IT A CERTAIN WAY.

Proper blocking should be a deflection, not a "block" as many students understand it. Any block is a combination of body positioning, body movement, and getting off line. Once you

CENTERLINE/BLOCK AND MOVE

Correct: weight 50/50.

Correct: cover centerline, transfer weight.

Correct: step, block, move body out of way.

understand these fundamentals, you can move on to using blocking in an offensive manner. By this we mean using it to disrupt an attacker's structure and rendering him incapable of attack after adjusting for the damage you have caused. Before you can do this, however, you must practice moving when an attack is launched. In time you will act almost preemptively. This is deflecting at its highest level.

Like an understanding of range, moving into safe or offensive distance while deflecting is not a "just pick it up as you go along" concept. If the elements that lead to deflection are not individually studied and understood, you will spend many years getting hit before you begin to comprehend it.

Specific Tips on Blocking

What we would like to do now is give you some nuts-and-bolts tips on blocking to help you see some of the more general points we have been making. Again, we're going to use generic hard styles as examples.

There are three categories of blocks: low, middle, and high. Within each of these there are different variations (for example: outside, inside, open hand).

Low Block

This is the first blocking technique to be practiced in karate, Tae Kwon Do, or in martial arts in general. It looks easy, but looks can be deceiving. This is a difficult block to master. Why practice low blocks? Because this technique contains the fundamentals of all blocks: timing, precision, positioning, and placement.

This technique is often considered the way to block kicks. Unfortunately, many of the errors we discussed regarding posture and positioning have stacked up here. The good news is that just as many errors have crept into the way most people kick as are encountered in this block.

As such, you might get away with a sloppy block against a sloppy kick. But against a correct kick, you will break your arm. Failing that, you still will get hit.

The common mistake of a student using low blocks is using his arm alone to block. It's not only painful, but ineffective. Your objective is to protect the front of your lower body—groin, solar plexus, and ribs. If you have a correct front stance, then your groin is protected. Dropping your elbow will automatically protect your ribs. Placing the block to the side of the attacker's leg, instead of the shin, is the ultimate objective.

The traditional drill of one-step sparring can mislead students into believing what they are learning is effective. Stepping back and executing the low block not only will result in a high risk of getting hit, but also creates a larger opening for your attacker.

PRACTICE HINT

Practice in front of a mirror and watch to see that your body is covered.

For example, a low block in a front stance with the left hand and with the right hand resting on the hip is a risky self-defense technique. Let's see what happens here: The defender's upper body is square and unprotected. His left hand is lower and his right hand is on the hip. This leaves the front of his body wide open. Students ought to be taught to practice bringing their hands to cover their front, even though the traditional way is to keep the nonblocking hand chambered.

REVERSE LOW BLOCK

The reverse low hand block is one of the most effective blocks in martial arts, yet only a few martial artists teach or practice it. Most martial artists know this technique, but do not practice it regularly.

> **PRACTICE HINT**
>
> Practice moving away when you block. Do not try to block a kick. Always try to deflect it.

Deflecting with your reverse hand is much more effective than with your forehand. For the purpose of illustration, we

Reverse low block.

position the would-be attacker at 12 o'clock. The reverse low block will force you to move away from 12 o'clock to 11 o'clock, thereby taking an angle away from the attack. The attacker's position will be on your line of counterattack, where he is forced to change direction to strike again. Most importantly, you will have secured your perimeter. This also allows a student to block without feeling as much pain as can occur in the traditional low block format. The reverse block will deflect a kick by a combination of moving away and redirecting the incoming attack. The hit is to the calf instead of the shin area.

Middle Block

There are many variations of blocking against a punch aimed at the solar plexus or face. Here we discuss the three most common middle blocks.

First is the forearm block (outside-inward) or chudan ude uke. Too many instructors may provide misinformation about part of this block. To top this, some rely on the myth that they can break an attacker's arm with this block—that would be far-fetched.

This block is designed to deflect the attacker's arm to the side so his forward motion slides straight past you. The deflection is just far enough so you don't get hit. At the same time, your hand is not far from your body, so you can use it to protect your front. Avoid overblocking! Be sure the elbow of the blocking arm is bent about 90 degrees. Your V form is very important. The forearm and the body should be aligned, with the elbow pointing straight down to the ground.

The fist of the blocking arm should be level with your chin and approximately eight inches in front of your body. Do not tense the muscles of your hand at the start of the block; it slows

MIDDLE BLOCK/TRIANGLE

Incorrect: weak triangle to compensate for bad placement.

Correct: proper triangle for proper placement.

Incorrect: weak triangle to compensate for bad placement.

down your movement. Tighten your muscles around your armpit at the moment of impact (this takes a lot of practice). Use the hip by rotating it toward the blocking arm.

The reverse outside-inward block is very risky. It is designed as an offensive technique. This is the only reverse block we do not advise practicing as a basic exercise.

Second is the forearm block (inside-outward) or chudan uchi uke. Again, this block is to deflect an attacker's punch to the side of the body. This kind of deflection will leave the attacker's body and your front wide open. Do not overblock! Make sure that you do not leave your blocking arm too far to the side. Your blocking elbow should be aligned with the side of your body. The other suggestions for the outside-inward forearm block are also applicable here.

The reverse inside-outward block is the most effective block of all. It can secure a large coverage area closer to the attacker's vital body section. It also puts the attacker in a difficult situation if he wants to launch the next move. The defender is in a good position and has ample opportunity to execute the next move instantly. This block is also very reliable. Reliability is a measure of success when evaluating how efficient the block is.

Third is the sword hand block or shuto uke. The edge of the hand is applied in a slantwise motion, as if we are trying to cut off the attacker's arm. The other arm is positioned in front of the solar plexus with palm facing up, so it can be used immediately

PRACTICE HINT

Make sure your arm is in the shape of a triangle.

SHUTO UKE

Correct: covering center line.

Shuto uke.

to counterattack or deflect. The blocking arm is the closest part of your body to the opponent. Be aware of this, since it can also be used for another deflection or attack. The blocking hand is brought forward and diagonally downward. Watch carefully how you execute this type of block. The blocking hand should pass over the forearm of the other hand. The other hand passes the elbow of the blocking arm. Remember V forms, always. Once again do not overblock; be sure that the arm does not go too far out, not beyond the side of your body. The other middle block points also can be used here.

Upper Level Block or Rising Block

This is the basic block to a counterattack and it is aimed above the solar plexus. From the lower-level block position, the left fist rises from under the right armpit, follows a half moon shape, and stops in front of the forehead. The common mistake of students executing the upper block is raising the blocking arm straight up. This creates a large opening. Your objective is to keep the elbow of the blocking arm at ninety degrees and complete the block with the forearm no more than ten centimeters in front of the forehead. The purpose is to sweep an upper-level strike upward or sideways.

Another common mistake is that many students do not place the elbow appropriately, resulting in a large frontal opening. The elbow should be placed where it can be used to deflect or protect the middle-level target effortlessly and in an instant. Less power should be used in the block. Your objective is not to meet the power of your opponent's strike with your block; instead strive to deflect the strike away from you or change the direction of the strike without feeling any resistance. This can only be achieved through regular practice. You must learn the technique with your body. Again, you must practice with a slower and wider range of motion first and then gradually add more speed and refine the technique to smaller movements. Focus on correct range, posture, and positioning before trying to add speed.

The reverse of this is one of the most effective blocks in martial arts. One of the benefits of the reverse high block is that the student will automatically move away from the straight line of 12 o'clock. At the same time, the attacker is forced to change direction to execute another attack. Therefore, the student has accomplished one of the required moves in his "not getting hit" goal. In the reverse upper level block, the student will benefit by creating a large opening in the attacker's side. It gives the student ample opportunity to counterattack, either with hands or kicks.

UPPER LEVEL/REVERSE UPPER LEVEL

No.   *Yes.*

No.   *Reverse.*

— 4 —

Punching

Fundamentals of Punching

Punching is both misunderstood and misapplied. The resulting mess is a compound problem of intent and technical flaws.

To help clarify some of the problems with intent, let's begin with a definition: punching is a closed-hand technique directed against a selected target that uses the action of muscles in the arms and trunk.

It is nothing more, nothing less. Punching is one tool among many that can be used to achieve a specific goal. It is not the first, middle, or last word in offense. It is part of a much larger, combined strategy that includes many other types of offenses, including grabs, pulls, traps, throws, and joint locks. We cannot stress the importance of this point enough. Understanding it will cause a major paradigm shift in your knowledge of offensive strategy.

You cannot, as many people do, punch and hope that it starts a cascade of beneficial results, including the hope that someone will stop attacking and run away because your punch hurt so much. Punching is not an end unto itself, nor is it some magical, mystical action that will solve all your problems. If you attempt to punch for any of these reasons, you have the wrong intent and won't be satisfied with the results. Worse, you will not be able to exploit the benefits and results that punches create.

You must punch to achieve a clearly defined tactical goal. The nature of this goal will dictate how much of your body weight is involved in the process. This short-term tactical goal is part of a much larger strategy. A punch is used to set up the next move. This is very much like a professional pool player whose every shot not only sinks a ball, but sets up the next one. He never just sends a ball into the pocket and then figures out what he is going to do next when the cue ball stops rolling. He plans ahead.

With this strategic aspect in mind, let's look at a more tactical definition: a punch is a way to deliver force into your opponent. If it doesn't do this, then you have technical problems, too.

The basic punching action is analogous to thrusting with a sword. It is from this correlation you learn fundamentals of punching, such as line, body mechanics, elbow use, foot placement, hip rotation, angle, and structure.

In the beginning, pretend your fist is the point of a sword that you are attempting to drive through your opponent's body. This will help you learn line, angle, and structure. The elbow is the sword hilt, and it must be in line with the tip to cleanly thrust through a mass. Another way of looking at it is that the force is your bullet, your fist is your front sight, your elbow your rear sight. The alignment of the sights determines where the bullet is going.

There are stages in learning how to punch. First, learn to punch from a neutral stance. The objective is to understand the

BASIC PUNCHING

Basic punching.

Correct.

particular motor skills involved. Learning from a neutral stance will isolate the technique, and it also teaches you reach.

One of the most important elements taught from punching in a neutral stance is the subtle hip movement (rotation/counter rotation) that makes powerful hits. Learning subtle movement is important because, upon hearing that the hips generate power, people tend to overcommit with their hips and shoulders to hit harder. Instead of making for a harder hit, this overcommitment robs you of power. You lose line direction of force, and the necessary structure to deliver it. With your feet planted, you cannot overcommit your hips.

A good punch depends on starting from a flexible posture and keeping the unnecessary muscle tension out of the arm and shoulder. The power of the move comes from the alignment of arm/elbow/shoulder and subtle hip movement, not strength.

The shortest distance between two points is a straight line. The movement of the hand and elbow must be in a straight line in upper, middle, and low punches. At the same time, the forearm lightly brushes the side of the body, and the forearm rotates inward. The upper punch should not be higher than the bridge of the nose.

The reason for focusing on these elements is that this simple punch is actually three. Three punches and three ranges. As it leaves your hip, it is an uppercut. As it goes a little farther, it rotates into a middle vertical punch. At the end, it is a horizontal punch. The idea of practicing this way is to make sure that you take full advantage of all possibilities.

Rotation is inherent in the entire movement, not just a last-minute snap. By rotating through the entire punch, you create a structure that is appropriate for the range. If you wait until the last second to snap out at the farthest reach, you don't have

PUNCHING

Correct.

Correct.

Correct.

Correct.

much structure until that time. If you have misjudged the range to your target impact point, your blow will not have power. By rotating throughout the move, no matter where you encounter the target impact point, you have structure and power.

Waiting for the end of the punch to rotate is not necessarily a fighting move, although it can be if the person has ranged the blow correctly. The snap at the end is more a display move for a competition kata. It greatly assists in creating the pop of a canvas gi sleeve that people mistakenly believe indicates power. Punching without structure is faster since it only involves the arm muscles and a fast-twitch response. This is good for point sparring, but it does not deliver force into your opponent, which is a fundamental goal of punching. Twisting and snapping at the end of a punch is an attempt to put structure back into the move. Unfortunately, without proper elbow position and body movement, this is a vain hope.

You also must work on not making a hard fist early on. Relax, then tighten the fist as it hits the target. This is an important component of understanding the multirange potential of a punch. You tighten at the point of impact, wherever that is, *not* at the end of the move. If you tighten your fist too early, it will affect the speed of your punch. Without speed, the punch cannot be expected to have much effect.

Once proper arm position and rotation are learned, the emphasis shifts to hip movement. By withdrawing the other arm as fast as possible, you will achieve the pairing of forces: pushing and pulling. This greatly assists in hip movement. Practice each of your style's punches from this neutral position to learn the subtle dynamics of these moves.

After you get a basic understanding of these concepts and applications, only then is it time to try to deliver the punch from different stances, i.e., free-fighting, front and L stances, and so forth. Now is the time to introduce combinations of different punches to give the student better options and opportunities.

Once these are learned, it is time to learn how to punch while moving into the stances. As you progress, you can work on hitting before you reach the new position and then hit again when you reach it. These are just some of the steps needed to learn the technical points of punching. Now let's look at some of its aspects.

Hip Rotation

Previously we spoke of placement, weight transfer, and range. It is moving your weight into the correct range that is the true source of power for punches, not, as many people believe, merely turning your hips. Having said that, however, it is important to know about hip rotation, too.

In delivering a punch, just as in hitting a baseball or making a tennis swing, the smooth, swift, and level turn of the hips is essential to the effective application of power. The power generated by the hips rotating is conveyed to the spine, then the chest and shoulders, and finally to the arm and fist. The turn of the hips produces the driving power necessary for a strong technique.

Hip rotation is not like a chunk of granite on a lazy Susan. Your body is not a solid piece of marble that swivels like a tank turret because your hips move. It is more of a snapping wave that rolls through your body.

Take a towel and roll it loosely from diagonal corner to diagonal corner (as though you were going to pop someone with it). Lay it on the floor and grasp one end. Give it a small flick and watch as the wave rolls down its length. That same kind of rolling force is what should pass through your body. From your hip twist it rolls up your spine, sweeps your shoulder forward, and then shoots out your punch.

Practice this move alone and don't try to retract yet. Nor should you attempt to strike with power at first. It is far more important to get the proper body mechanics through structure and relaxation. You will not be able to create this wave unless you are relaxed, and you cannot relax if you are not in the proper position. This is why you need to focus on only one aspect before moving on to retraction. There is much to learn right here.

Once you can generate a smooth, forward-flowing wave, then you can create retraction through hip rotation. Take the rolled towel and flick it like a whip. The same physics that send a wave rolling out, bring it back. The whip crack occurs when you bring it back, and it doesn't transpire from strength. No matter how hard you try to throw that towel out, it won't work if you don't create rolling waves—both going out and coming back. This same principle applies in your hip rotation.

It doesn't take much hip turn to create a wave. Most people make a mistake by overcommitting. What it does take is practice, creating the outbound wave and the retraction to produce the whip-crack power delivery. You must practice the subtle timing of sending the wave out and then beginning retracting hip rotation before your fist reaches the target impact point. As the timing is subtle, so, too, must be your hip movement. If it is too large, you will never get the proper timing.

Myths of Punching

This is a good time to address several myths about punching.

MYTH: THE MUCH TOUTED ONE-PUNCH, ONE-KILL IDEA.

The sad reality is if you try to make any punch your one-stop answer, you start compounding errors. This idea of one-punch, one-kill is based on the mythologies that have arisen about ancient warriors being able to punch through armor and cave in the chest of an opponent. Although few people believe killing an opponent by using only one mighty blow is possible, students are trained to block, counterattack, and stop. The unstated assumption is that if they were to execute the blow hard enough, it would stop any further aggression.

The fallacy of this idea is proved in every professional boxing match. Even there, knockouts are relatively rare. They only occur after a flurry of blows have already been thrown and only when very specific conditions have been created. If in boxing, perhaps the highest refinement of punching, the participant can't drop an opponent with only one punch, how can a martial arts student believe it is that easy?

Yet this myth still doggedly hangs on. It is, in fact, encouraged by poorly understood one-step training. The problem with this is that such thinking encourages tactical, rather than strategic, ideas of punching. If you expect one punch to do all your work, you will stop. You also have sacrificed any chance of strategic movement and have set yourself up to be hit. We say this because in attempting to generate enough force to make this "killer blow," most people take a deep, rooted stance that is difficult to move from when counterattacked by an opponent's multiple attacks.

MYTH: THE MYTH OF "NUCLEAR BOMB" PUNCHING.

This is a close cousin to the one-punch, one-kill myth. The reason we call it this is because the student thinks that his powerful blow is a nuclear bomb. That is to say, it doesn't matter where it lands, the whole city will be destroyed.

The truth is the human body is somewhat armored against impacts, especially from the front. The placement of bones and muscle give us a degree of protection against a blow. A poorly aimed punch will bounce off, even with multiple hits, if poorly targeted. Most of your blows will bounce or deflect off your opponent with little effect beyond inflicting some pain.

Having said this, like real armor, there are chinks. These are vital targets that are vulnerable, far more painful, and likely to disrupt your opponent's structure when struck. Any punch you throw will be much more effective if it is targeted to one of the vital areas.

Instead of trying to nuke your opponent, make your blows like precision-guided missiles that strike vital targets. One well-aimed punch can have the effect of three poorly aimed, but heavier, hits. One-punch, one-kill, and nuclear hitting are both fantasy expectations.

The problem with fantasy attacks in one style is that the rebuttal solutions of another style are just as unreliable and unrealistic. If one-punch, one-kill is on one end of the fantasy spectrum chain punching on the same line (straight blast) is on the other end. The idea behind this is that you charge in with a flurry of punches that overwhelm your opponent.

In reality, only a few people in the world can apply this multitasking effort effectively against a skilled opponent. Putting it bluntly, the success of this strategy is largely dependent on having a rather "thick" or inexperienced opponent. Just because you have seen it work in the academy against new or junior students don't believe it will work against an opponent who still has his wits about him.

When your mind is set to do chain punching, your body will go straight forward. If your opponent is stupid enough to stay in one place or step straight back, then chain punching might have a chance of hitting the target. Most people, however, will eventually move to the side or muster a counterattack. While your action continues straight forward, your opponent will have your side wide open and close. This is too risky and too dangerous.

Realistically, the reason this maneuver is successful is that many people do not understand the movement aspect of blocking, so it is your opponent's lack of experience that makes it work. Another reason it is thought to work, especially in "real fights," is the tendency of an attacker to grab an opponent and, holding him in place, proceed to pummel him. In both cases, you will see that the victim is overwhelmed not because he is "beaten down" but because he trips while trying to backpedal.

A continuous flurry of blows will either overwhelm your opponent or begin to lose their effectiveness, and the result is usually the latter. The reason we say this is because unless someone is extremely skilled, the caliber of his blows will degrade the more he tries to chain. The longer you try to punch, the less effective you become. The real problem with this strategy is that in light of this decay, sooner or later your victim—if he doesn't trip—is going to retaliate. If you are so busy focusing on all the things you are doing to him, you are going to leave yourself open to what he is about to do to you.

Chain punching is not really a strategy, it is a repeating tactic. Because it is not a real strategy, very seldom can the person who is chain punching make the shift to true strategic thinking and exploit the reactions he has created. Instead of doing another move that would quickly end the altercation, he will often continue trying to jackhammer his opponent into submission.

MYTH: A SPORT PUNCH ONLY HAS TO BE DONE HARDER TO TURN IT INTO A POWERFUL BLOW.

As we stated in the previous chapter, there is a big difference between sport punching and punching for power. That difference is simple to understand: structure. Sport punching relies on speed and has very little structure involved. Power punching relies on moving your body and delivering that momentum through structure.

Although we call it sport punching, competitive kata also has had a serious effect on compounding problems with punching. The further away from combat application "show" kata has gone (for example, cartwheels, backflips, and other gymnastics), the flashier and less realistic punches have become. The difference between the two is like the difference between shooting a gun in the movies and actual combat shooting. In a movie, you don't have to hit a target, you just have make it look good.

The reason show and sport punches are so fast is that they only have to involve the arm. There is little need for the elbow to be in the correct position or for the body to move. You just shoot it out.

Unlike show or sports, punching to deliver power must have structure and momentum. It also requires moving into range, which takes more time. A powerful punch takes longer because you must coordinate several aspects.

Full contact and boxing straddle these two extremes. But these systems spend considerable time training to perfect both speed and power hitting. They also specifically train for ring strategy, which combines both ways of hitting. The key component for that, however, is the emphasis on strategy within the parameters of the sport. Comparatively few schools train for semipro or professional fighting these days.

Moving on, let's talk about the different types of punches. Depending on what style you practice, they can range from few (boxing only has five basic punches) to many (all the different hand positions of various animal forms in Chinese Wushu).

Rather than go into details, we will give you three key components to punching effectively. The first, as we already mentioned, is the alignment of the fist and elbow with both moving down the "line of force" of your punch. This also greatly assists in preventing the student from bending his wrist slightly when he punches.

The second is the proper location of your elbow in relationship to your body. You want your elbow to be positioned so it can deliver your body's momentum through the blow. Generally, with straight hits you want it in between your body and your opponent's body. If you are punching straight, you don't want your elbow off to the side. Of course, this changes with the direction you are moving. For example, with hooks your elbow is up and out, but your body is moving the same way as the blow.

Proper elbow position is essential to maintaining the structure to hit with power. In the same way that you tested your blocking poses by having someone push against them, you can check your punching postures to see if they are structurally solid or if they wiggle, wobble, and collapse when pressure is applied.

The third component is your shoulder. Pay close attention to its rise and fall. Often a mere matter of inches can rob you of structure. By dropping your shoulder for certain punches, you remove its tendency to flex under pressure (sometimes up to three inches).

Paying attention to these three components and experimenting with how pressure affects them will teach you much about finding the proper posture—and by extension, structure—of punching. Your entire arm should not flex, bow, or wobble when you punch.

Because "sport" punching has been both overemphasized and bastardized, there is a great deal of confusion about correct techniques. While there is nothing technically wrong with sport hitting, the student must know the difference between it and punching for power.

The student must research correct punching techniques for the situation. Although we are not fans of fragmented training, this may be appropriate for your situation. As such, you must do what works for where you are. In sports, hit sports. In demo, hit demo. In kata, hit kata. In fighting, hit fighting. Still better though is to understand the range, posture, position, and placement of each.

Just remember, a powerful punch takes time to deliver, so don't rush it. In training or in the ring, learn to make sure your component parts are present. In time and with study, they will automatically be there. By focusing on putting them in, you can drop aspects you consciously choose to omit (for example, for the protection of a sparring partner or safety of a student).

Intentionally dropping one of these elements will allow you to control the amount of force you are applying. Instead of unintentionally losing power through poor posture, you are consciously using the same physics as a safety measure.

Striking

Striking is a close cousin to punching. If a punch can be considered a sword thrust, the striking movement is analogous to slashing, using the power of the arm. The striking force is transmitted laterally with the elbow, forearm, or both. Open-hand strike (shuto), open-hand backhand, and palm heel strikes are the most commonly used in the arts of self-defense. When employing strikes, your objective is to hit the target and let your hand pass by so you can reuse the same hand to block, attack, or return to a ready position without wasted motion. It is obvious that if you have the ability to strike accurately, the defender has no need to block because you've already hit the target. In this sense, the art of striking is one of the most important techniques in martial arts.

Some students develop bad habits of not returning to a ready position after delivering the attack. Other students return straight back to chamber after each strike and leave opportunities for opponents to attack. You can practice by hitting in the air and flowing into ready position or you may hit a bag to develop wrist strength. Each has advantages and disadvantages.

The proper introduction of this technique for most students is as one strike from a natural stance. They then progress to a strike from a horse stance. Students are advised to hold their elbows close to their sides, tense their legs, and tighten their stomach at the moment of impact. This is fundamental training.

Many instructors do not understand error detection, therefore, they repeat the same basic practice year after year. Two things might come out of these habits:

1. Without something to hit you will develop speed but not power delivery or an understanding of range. You might

increase your speed, power, and understanding of range if you are practicing on a bag. Hitting the bag has many benefits. One, that no one discusses or that is not being told because the instructor doesn't know it, is properly hitting to strengthen your wrist at the moment of impact. Many martial arts students injure their hand after hitting the target, be it bag or person.

2. Despite the advantages of practicing diligently, you might develop the bad habit of leaving your hand where your last strike was. In other words, you don't rechamber. An alert instructor will see and correct this immediately. Other students have the bad habit of punching straight and then chambering. Consequently, they create an opening for their opponents and need to take too much effort to reuse the striking hand. Both your hands should remain in the front of your body, forming a L, after or before the strike. This will provide protection, as well as readiness for the next movement.

Until now we have largely focused on the more technical aspects of punching and striking; now let's look at some of the common misconceptions and their counterpoint realities.

Some of the realities of striking are:

REALITY: HE AIN'T GONNA STAND THERE.

Many schools train students to do preset series of attacks, commonly called chaining, combos, or a school-specific term. The problem with how these are commonly taught is the imaginary opponent either does not move at all or magically comes into range for the next strike. Especially common in modern interpretations of kata is long-range punches and kicks, immediately followed by short-range strikes—without moving forward to adjust for the range of the next blow. Consider this for a moment: Assuming the first blow was effective, your opponent would be knocked which way? Backwards! How are you going to be able to deliver short-ranged blows from this new range?

With any technique, what you will do next needs to be dictated by your attacker's responses—not by a sequence of moves you have learned by rote. This is why you must consider the range, posture, position, and placement of every punch within your system. Then analyze your katas, forms, drills, and combos in light of these standards. Is the next move feasible?

Furthermore, you must experiment with the reactions that these moves actually produce. Does the move work as advertised in practice? Does the person's body move the way it is supposed to when you perform the move? Is he set up for the next strike in the combo? Or do additional elements and small tweaks need to be added to the basic move? (You should know, it is these small—but critical—elements to set up the next move that are most commonly lost in some commercialized systems).

These are the variables you have to consider when the move is even partially successful. But what if he counters, blocks, counterattacks, or does something unexpected? Like attacking you first? That is where you really need to have invested time in learning range, positioning, placement, and posture instead of just combos. These are what secure your perimeter and prevent you from being exposed.

If you fall into bad habits such as chambering during a fight, not returning to the ready position, or not securing your perimeter, chances are good that you will get hit before you can land an attack of your own. Your first reaction of the way to use your strike will be dictated by your position and placement in response to the attacker.

If you assume your attacker will stand toe-to-toe with you, you are creating a big problem for yourself. A boxer will stay toe-to-toe with you because he learns to fight in close. That range will take away any kick's effectiveness. In this situation, you have to two choices: control the distance or step off the straight line. Otherwise, by virtue of two hits out of three, you will get hit.

MARTIAL MUSINGS

As a student of the martial arts, I have observed, and experienced firsthand, the techniques of boxers. The way the boxer uses his hands is much better, in my opinion, than that of the karate or Tae Kwon Do student. Most good boxers are light on their feet because they are masters of weight transfer; their positioning is good and their placement is excellent. Their style of attack and counter-attack is great. Their jabs are as important as their primary punches. Unlike martial arts students, boxers are taught from the start to act naturally with their jabs. Their disadvantage is their lower body, since, by the nature of their sport, the lower body target is not allowed. So, I can say that their weaknesses are lower body protection.

—Tristan Sutrisno.

Punching

REALITY: YOU NEED BODY MOVEMENT, STRUCTURE, AND RANGE TO HIT HARD.

You need accuracy—not speed—to hit effectively. Most people stiffen when you tell them to hit hard with speed. Because of this, you are hitting slower and with less power.

We need to learn how and what kind of reach we can achieve with kicks or punches. Understanding distance will help you tremendously in increasing your speed and power. Remember, the more speed, the more powerful the impact. Trying to attain power first, then speed, is not effective because you will stiffen and slow yourself.

Try this one: Hold your fist tightly, then punch a hanging bag. Compare it with not making a fist until the moment of impact. You will feel and see that hitting the bag with a relaxed hand increases the speed and power.

REALITY: NO MATTER HOW WELL YOU FLOW, IF YOU ARE FLOWING INTO THE WRONG PLACE OR ARE UNABLE TO HIT THE CORRECT TARGET YOU WILL NOT ACHIEVE YOUR GOALS.

Targets also determine speed and power of impact. The target of the punch should not be higher than the bridge of your nose. Your objective is to hit the target with the first two knuckles of your fist. Anything higher than the bridge of your nose will force your fingers to hit the target first, consequently hurting both you and the target. If you drive a car up a hill, you must push the pedal deeper to get more juice. It would be the same if you are going to punch higher—you have to insert more power, energy, and speed. Just remember that any time you are using an upper punch above your range, you also will leave your body wide open. Beware of it.

Learn to punch from wherever your hand was last with the same energy as punching from the waist line. This is a very common mistake for martial artists who are taught to punch from a constant chambered position. As mentioned before, punching from the waist is basically used to learn how to execute punches. Later on, you will have to learn how to punch from any position with the same intensity and effort. Many students get stuck at the first level, only adding intensity, speed, and power when their punches come from the waist.

REALITY: MOST DOJO-TRAINED FIGHTERS HAVE A HABIT OF MOVING ONLY ONCE AND THEN ATTACKING FROM THE SAME POSITION.

This is what we might call a harsh reality. It is harsh because it can be detrimental to the practitioner. This habit arises out of ippon kumite during class or point sparring in class or tournaments. This habit must be broken. Learning the important elements of this art include learning about and understanding rhythm, timing, and distance. Although you should learn to spot this error, it takes hands-on guidance by a teacher who understands the concept of error detection.

~ 5 ~

Stances

Fundamentals of Stances

Stances (base) are transitional—you take them for a purpose and for the moment. They are not, as many seem to believe, statue poses from kata nor are they something you "take" and then "fight from." They most especially are not something you learn for kata and then forget about in sparring. The way most people jump nervously straight back and forth in sparring shows their lack of understanding about stances. They fail to strategically apply stances. With stances thrown out the window, so go correct body movement, stability, and what it takes to generate power.

Stances are one of the most important parts of martial arts. They are the very groundwork of any movement. Without them, there is *no* art. Stance is the base from which you launch the attack, where you retreat, where you move to avoid a conflict, and where you build the defensive/offensive perimeter. You must have a good, solid stance before you attempt to execute any technique. Your base will dictate whether you come out victorious, with or without battle. Beyond winning or losing, it can dictate your survival.

Stance is the base, but it's also mobile. It can be moved or held, depending on the purposes. Stances are like a helicopter that transports a recon team to the landing zone. It can stay in one place and fire its guns, or drop the team in time for them to finish the job. Or it can move the soldiers to a more advantageous landing zone to do the job. Stance is not designed as a weapon: you add the weapon to it. The primary job of a stance is as a support team. Its task is to make sure the strike force has everything needed to accomplish the mission.

A skilled martial artist cleverly uses stances to his advantage. If the needs of the moment change, you adapt by changing your stance. Your base or stance varies with the situation. It is this multifaceted nature of stances that has not been taught to many martial artists. This failure to understand stances largely arises from the "damming the river" mindset that has crept into how katas are performed ("stop-and-take-a-picture" poses). If you dam the flow of movement, then, yes, stances become dead statue poses with little value in either sparring or fighting. That is where jitterbugging takes over. [Some of today's martial artists have atrophied kata and then tried to ape boxers—but do not understand the nuances of either.] As a good boxer fights from the bottom of his feet, so, too, does a good martial artist.

Stances give us base, structure, and mobility. They provide choices and options. They allow us to control range, cover distance, safely put our body weight into a move, keep us balanced, allow for effective offense and defense, and keep our retreats organized and secured, instead of becoming routs. All this comes from knowing how to move from stance to stance in reaction to what is happening at the moment.

If we are standing in a natural stance, with the body weight equally shared by both legs (50/50) when attacked, we can stay in the same stance and respond with our hands, move to another direction and take the same stance (evade), move and change the stance (immediately move into a tactical position), or, although more risky, step back and prepare to defend ourselves (fighting stance).

You might not be in any type of stance when forced to take action. Sometimes you are sitting down or standing without a proper stance, meaning you might be hunching, bending, and so forth. If someone attacks you in this situation, you might respond with your weapons first, meaning your hand initiates a defensive action, then you flow into a stance to support it. Or you move your body to safety before responding with a counter-attack. Another possibility is to continue with defensive moves, such as block/deflect and evasion/avoidance techniques. Still another solution is to do defensive handwork to cover your movement into an offensive position.

No matter what option you choose, you will end up in stances. If you don't consciously focus on learning how to flow into a proper, structural stance, you will find yourself weak and vulnerable. You cannot effectively generate or deal with force from that kind of pose.

You are always either in a stance or transitioning between them. Whether that is launching an offense or a defensive move or preparing to step into another stance doesn't matter. What counts is that you are moving your weight.

The skill of weight transfer is of vital importance when transitioning between stances, especially during free fighting. This is when the elements of position, placement, and distance must all come together and coordinate with weight transfer. You may observe at tournaments that many martial arts students do not have a clear understanding of weight transfer together with range and distance. They stay in one fixed stance or continuously move back and forth, without clear weight transfer.

Without understanding the importance of weight transfer in stances it is not only difficult to deliver a variety of effective attacks, but also is a constant drain on stamina. It is not difficult to tell when their attack is coming because they often stop to plant their weight before they attack. Because their stance is fixed, there are limited options open for their attacks.

Intense practice and focus must be devoted to practicing moving your body weight subtly and smoothly within a stance while maintaining it. A drill we do is to have a student practice moving his or her weight 100 percent from leg to leg while walking in a forward stance. You have students check the completeness of the transfer by having them lift the light foot. When the student can do it without having to shift the last few inches or without teetering to stay upright, the correct posture has been achieved. This is an extreme position and is a place beyond which the student does not want to pass. Awareness of this outer limit must be ingrained for proper movement.

The reason we say this posture is an extreme is because you do not want to overshoot it while moving. If you do, you will lose balance and structure. If you take your weight past this point, you will start to wobble and have to counterbalance—not exactly something you want to do while trying to avoid an attack.

Although you can get away with undershooting this position when stepping or walking, you can't if you are trying to kick with power. Unfortunately, in attempting to generate fast kicks, many so-called advanced martial artists start their kicks before achieving this position. In fact, it is not uncommon for people doing this to divert a large amount of their kicking power into moving their body weight the rest of the way over the supporting leg. Instead of transferring their weight and then kicking near the end of the transfer (so the kick delivers the body's momentum), the first part of their kick is what finishes their weight transfer. Then their leg pops out without any of the body's momentum.

You can deliver a punch without changing your stance from start to finish (weight transfer only) or strike while stepping forward into a stance (stepping, weight transference, and striking all at once). You can slide your foot out into position and then transfer your weight and strike as you move into the stance. It doesn't matter how you do it. In all cases, you will be back in a stance when the blow is delivered.

If you take nothing else from this chapter, remember that stances are a way to manifest weight transfer, position, posture, and placement. They are the helicopters that deliver your strike force to the aforementioned landing zone (position), so they can easily reach the object and deliver the fire mission (placement). Without correct stances to give you structure, without an understanding of weight transfer (and stance use) within, and without understanding the effect stances have on range, your control over force is gone. You will not be able to effectively generate or handle incoming force. Without force, martial arts is just dancing.

Types of Stances

There are many types of stances. For the purpose of this book, we selected four of the most commonly used in hard-style martial arts. These are not fighting stances; they are training stances or stances used for a specific purpose. You don't start fighting from a front stance.

1. **Natural stance**—The body weight is equally distributed on both legs (50/50). This is a relaxed stance where a person can instantly and easily move in any direction. In all stances, the distance between the left and right legs is shoulder width. It's like walking on both rails of a railroad track—the feet are constantly separated at the same width. We teach our students to be cautious where they choose to stand, so the location will not hinder or prevent them from moving freely. We teach them not to become immobilized. Their body, legs, and hands should be free and able to move instantly.

    The guard stance also is 50/50, but it is in a slightly sideways position. A difference is that usually in natural stance both hands are down. In a guard stance, both hands are up in position to respond with defensive or offensive movements.

    The reason we don't call this a fighting stance is because it isn't. You aren't fighting—yet. It is really a "ready to fight" stance. A fighting stance is what you move into to create or deal with an attack.

2. **Front stance**—The feet move into position and body weight is transferred to 85 percent on the front leg and 15 percent on the back leg. The big toe on the front leg is pointed to 12 o'clock, while the heel is pointed to 8 o'clock. The knee has enough bend that you can't see your front toe, and the shin is perpendicular to the floor. The front knee is angled somewhat to protect the groin, unless the attack comes in from 1 o'clock to 3 o'clock. In that case, hand positioning is critical in a front stance.

The back leg is straight, but the knee is not locked. The feet are shoulder width apart as though you were walking on railroad tracks. Like railroad tracks, the width of your shoulder doesn't vary. The distance from the heel of your front foot to the tip of your rear foot's big toe is one and a half times the width of your shoulders.

The position of the rear foot is somewhat different. Your little toe would be on 3 o'clock while your heel would be on 5, so your knee is pointing forward. This gives you all kinds of advantages. It allows for forward steps or kicks. It also allows ease in stepping backwards.

If your rear foot's big toe is pointing toward noon, it puts too much strain on your knee and automatically locks it while shifting your weight forward. If your rear foot's big toe is pointed off at a 90-degree angle from noon, your knee is pointing in the wrong direction to step forward. You are likely to be pushed over the side of your foot by a heavy rush, since you have to turn your foot before you can step. This foot position also shifts the bulk of your weight forward.

The front stance is very flexible and can used to teach defensive moves such as block/deflect; avoidance by moving; changes in direction (positioning); or offensive moves to deliver counterattacks or to attack first.

3. **Back stance**—This is a defensive position and a temporary stance. Many martial arts instructors won't agree with the statement since they teach their students to punch from a back stance position. Can it be done? Yes, but it is a very limited and possibly painful move because you can strain your muscles when trying to generate power. Since

the hip is already square to the front, the punch gets its strength from the shoulder only, with no hip twist to help generate force.

Back stance.

The range of such a punch is also much shorter compared to blocking from a back stance, sliding into a front stance, and counterattacking with a reverse punch, for instance. Shifting into a front stance also allows weight transfer, which generates a more powerful blow.

In a back stance, your front foot's toe points to 12 o'clock and your back leg's toe points to 3 o'clock. Both knees are slightly bent. Body weight is 65 percent on the back leg and 35 percent on the front leg. The upper body is perpendicular to the floor (standing straight up).

Usually this is accompanied with open- or sword-hand blocks. By transferring your weight back from a front stance, you negate the range of your opponent's attack by moving his target (you). Also with some practice, you can transform this stance into a grab and pull.

You should not attempt to kick with your front leg from a back stance without a definite weight transfer first. If you use your rising leg as a means to transfer your weight, much of the energy that could go into the kick is wasted in the weight shift.

Cat stance.

4. Cat stance—This stance can be defined as an offensive stance. It gives you an opportunity to kick or block with your front leg. Your body weight rests 95 percent on the back and 5 percent on the front leg. The back foot is pointed to 3 o'clock. The front leg rests on the ball of the foot with the heel off the floor. Both legs are slightly bent. This is the smaller version of the back stance, except in the ball of the foot placement and weight distribution.

Hand position is critical in this stance. Since this stance is offensive, your posture must be such that your hands are good to go without unnecessary movement.

You can easily move and change directions in the cat stance. When blocking with the left hand, you can usually maintain the ball of the foot position with the heel off the floor. To counterattack with a punch, we suggest either dropping the heel to the floor so the hip can freely rotate to give maximum impact, or sliding the front leg to a front stance and at the same time combining the weight transfer and hip rotation to achieve a devastating reverse punch. In a cat stance, you can use your left hand to measure range by doing a jablike motion and following with a right hand attack or kick. In all these techniques, changing the stance is required.

These four stances are positions you move into by transferring your weight and stepping. The ability to flow smoothly from one to another is dependent on your understanding of weight transference and your skill at weight management.

In the beginning, and to teach the importance of weight transfer, students should be taught "coming to center." This is the deliberate overemphasis of shifting your weight entirely over one leg before stepping. The student's arms and legs are pulled in close and poised to move into the next posture/stance. This action brings all the student's weight into one tight, concise package. Then students step out into whatever stance/posture they are practicing. By consciously moving this way, the student also learns not to bob up and down and change height.

Stances

COMING TO CENTER

From ready stance shift weight onto one leg.

Extend foot to proper position.

Transfer weight.

Move into stance.

The knees are bent to maintain a constant level under the instructor's watchful eye.

In time, when the student can demonstrate smooth, flowing weight management, he or she can begin "shaving" the weight transfer while moving from stance to stance. This is to say that the person can experiment with other variations of weight management. But this should not be done until full weight transfer is achieved smoothly and fluidly.

— 6 —

Kicking Techniques

Film, television, inexperienced instructors, and certain sports styles promote high kicks as the ultimate weapon of the martial arts—the higher, the better. This is false information. Many instructors and students are so impressed with high kicks that one of their main objectives in learning the arts is to master kicking techniques.

Kicking is an important part of learning the martial arts. A kick is more powerful than a punch and can achieve greater effects. It allows us to operate at a farther range. We also know that executing a correct kick requires more use of muscles, energy, and concentration than executing a punch, which makes it more difficult, too.

What many do not notice, however, is that to kick with power, you need weight transfer, balance, structure, timing, coordinated body movement, and a thorough understanding of range. You can operate without these, but you won't be kicking with power, nor will you be kicking effectively.

Let's start by looking at a major source of errors.

High Kicks

How effective is high kicking? The answer to this question depends on how you determine effectiveness.

High kick.

In a tightly controlled ring, with strict rules about allowable targets and techniques with lots of time and as a means to unnerve an opponent, they work wonderfully. Outside of those limited circumstances, things begin to unravel.

We understand and agree this is a controversial statement. But look at it from a practical standpoint: High kicks have created all sorts of problems about understanding kicking in general. In rushing to get to these flashy, impressive kicks, the fundamentals often are ignored.

We are not impressed with high kicks because we have seen and experienced their miserable failure in a real fight. An experienced fighter who can control range and understands the weaknesses of high kicks will step in and strike your groin hard enough to make you look like a squirrel with nuts stuffed in your cheeks. Now the really bad news: that's the least that can happen. Important things tend to break when you hit the ground from that pose.

Considering how hard it is to execute a high kick and the fact that it offers little in return, it's safe to say it is beautiful in the dojo, but not productive in a real encounter. This is because its success relies on four elements: (1) correct range (hard to control against a fast opponent); (2) an opponent ignorant of trapping and leverage; (3) lots of space (such kicks are useless in a crowded environment such as a nightclub, restaurant, and so forth); (4) a stable, smooth, nonslick surface (ice, slippery floors, loose rocks, and uneven footing will cause all kinds of problems unless your form is absolutely perfect).

SWOT Analysis

We have come to this conclusion about high kicks' effectiveness based on SWOT analysis—strength, weaknesses, opportunity, and threat:

Strength—If executed properly a lower kick's powerful and longer reach can be a big surprise to your opponent.

Weaknesses—Requires a lot of energy and precision, needs a superb weight transfer, easily misses the target, environment dictates how you can execute it, clothing provides advantages or disadvantages. Since the high kick's target is the head area, which is a smaller object, the defender can easily avoid it with a slight movement. Each time you deliver a high kick, you leave your body wide open. If you do not chamber your kick quickly, you will be in big trouble. A high kick requires maximum energy and a longer route to the target. Imagine you are driving on a flat road at 55 miles an hour. Your leg stays comfortably on the gas pedal. Suddenly, there's a hill in front of you. To maintain the same speed, you have to push the pedal harder to gain more energy and power. That's the same with the high kick. To maintain the speed to reach the high target, you have to increase your energy. Caution: Not everyone can deliver a perfect high kick and knock someone out—just like in the movies.

Opportunity—Understanding the target, adjusting the target, and using the opportunity of longer range to your advantage in a well-executed *low* kick.

Threat—Without awareness of the above weaknesses, martial artists who have trained in high kicks will face grave danger in a real situation. A high kick can look beautifully artistic and gymnastically acrobatic, but it is still a high risk. If executed perfectly—meaning impeccable speed and timing, judgment of distance, and in the perfect environment that lends itself to the kick's usage—it will result in a high return. The target is hit with a full force that can knock a person out, or at the very least stun him for a second or two.

SWOT is an invaluable tool for error detection. Take the SWOT checklist and test every technique you know against it. Running your technique through this process is like debugging computer code: you run the debugger and see where things hang up.

Many errors will reveal themselves in the increased time it takes to prepare for a move. That is to say, the steps necessary to execute a technique have no effect on your opponent's ability to attack you while you are doing them. For example, in a four-stage process, nothing significant happens to your opponent until step 4. This is both a weakness and a result of one, two, three, . . . nine, ten thinking, where the critical middle stages have been lost, but the form remains. Go back to the Heian 3 example in chapter 1. The loss of a grab in the kata created incredible weakness in the technique. You cannot rely on your opponent waiting patiently for you to complete your four-stage technique.

SWOT application is not negative or debunking. It is more a defining process. It is learning and understanding the proper applications of a technique. When you understand the correct time and way to apply a technique, by extension you will also know when not to use it. SWOT helps you determine these factors.

Non–Martial Art Reasons for High Kicks

Having said all this, why are high kicks popular? Well, these whiz bang, flashy moves appeal to young, flexible, and healthy kids with good knees. For the younger children, it is the Power Rangers and Teenage Mutant Ninja Turtles all rolled into one. As one instructor describes them, they are everything that children get yelled at for doing at home—running, leaping about, screaming, and flailing wildly. Such behavior is not only condoned, but encouraged, and high kicks are part of that.

For the older teenagers, well, speaking frankly, no other martial art technique so resembles the Masai courtship dance. This is where young Masai warriors line up and impress members of the opposite sex by how high they can jump. All it takes is one glance at the gaggle of teenagers off in a corner during a belt test break to see the accuracy of this analogy. Fortunately for the dignity of the martial arts school, the puffing of the cheeks and cyclic droning the Masai engage in while courting is not included in this display of teenage physical prowess.

High kicks also have another advantage for older instructors. It's an open secret among senior instructors that high kicks are the martial arts equivalent of sending the kids to the movies. It not only gives them something to do, but it keeps them busy for hours. On top of that, it wears them out and makes them more manageable.

All flippancy aside, high kicks also greatly assist youngsters in gaining kudos during demonstrations and winning trophies in nontraditional kata competitions. All of this is great for building a young person's self-esteem.

However, stories about flying kicks taking warriors off horses, or these kicks being useful for self-defense should be discouraged because young people often believe these myths. They may try to use such moves in real situations, with very unpleasant results.

Preparation to Kick

Kicking is an integral part of learning the martial arts. As a matter of fact, without knowing how to do kicks, your movements probably look somewhat like a drunken and funny boxer.

Delivering a good kick requires a smooth weight transfer, since you will be transferring all your weight to one leg while the other is kicking.

Kickers also have to control and balance their entire body. Any slight movement will deflect the kick's direction and effectiveness.

As a preparatory drill to learning how to kick, we recommend that you have your students practice weight transfer in a neutral stance. This is a 100 percent transfer from foot to foot. Once the weight is 100 percent on one foot, have the student lift the light foot—without any extra movement or weight transfer. At first have the student just lift his or her foot and move it into various positions around the supporting knee. The goal is for the student to be able to do this without wobbling, counterbalancing, leaning, or adjusting. Once students can do this with ease, have them move their knees into kicking position. Unless it is absolutely necessary for the kick, do not have them twist their hips yet.

This very simple drill isolates two of the most common errors in how most people kick: bad weight transfer and weak balance. By focusing on these factors, you will not only increase the effectiveness of your students' kicks, but will address those errors, too.

Due to the lack of understanding and even less emphasis on teaching weight transfer, many people—including a number of paper masters—rely on what we call the tornado effect to remain upright. This movement sucks your weight into a spiraling vortex/decaying orbit. Your hips' circular motion spirals you into balance. We use the word balance with great reservation because it is not true equilibrium. You stay upright but are simply orbiting around the spot where balance would be. It is not balance keeping you upright, but rather centrifugal force. Balance would be your body weight rotating on a vertical axis (a planted leg).

What you really are doing is slinging yourself around an anchoring point (very much like swinging on a rope tied to a tree branch). If you were to stop moving, you'd fall. If you are in balance and you stop, you simply stop spinning and remain in position. Balance doesn't rely on movement; it's there or it isn't.

TORNADO EFFECT

Incorrect: ready.

Incorrect: using the hip twist to transfer weight and keep balance.

Incorrect: out of control.

This use of centrifugal force has been called dynamic balance. In a nutshell, the idea is that you use this slinging action and rely on your opponent's face to stop your motion (not unlike using a backstop to catch a thrown ball). It is arguable that kicking in this manner is slightly faster—especially for inexperienced kickers. But the idea is exactly why so many inexperienced kickers fall into this bad habit.

Putting it bluntly, tornado effect kicking (or dynamic balance, if you will) is a point-sparring move only. Even then, it is a bad habit to get into. Most deaths and serious injuries in the sparring ring occur from head injuries from falls (this, more than protecting your pretty face, is why head gear should be worn). If your anchoring foot slips or if your weight is being sent too far out (misjudging range and trying to reach), you are going to fall. How many times have you seen people in a sparring match fall while trying to kick? This is why. They didn't lose their balance, they lost their anchor. This is like the branch your rope is tied to breaking as you swing.

You also will fall if, when you are using the tornado effect, your opponent doesn't block, but instead deflects. His mass will not be there as a backstop to catch your force. Think about how many times you have seen someone fall when their kick is deflected. If you could rewind and watch, what you would often see is that the blocker moved to either 11 o'clock or 1 o'clock. You will see these kinds of falls even in professional matches, which shows you how prevalent the tornado effect has become.

The tornado effect is not a good idea in any fighting situation because you are not in balance. If you are struck, body checked, miss your target, or your opponent knows how to shed force or deflect, you have a good chance of falling. Even if you don't fall, you will end up wasting precious time trying to regain your balance.

Correct: Weight transfer before twist maintains balance.

There are three other reasons why your students should be proficient at this weight transfer/balance drill before attempting to kick. First, it increases the power of their kicks. What people don't realize about tornado kicks is that although they are possibly faster for the inexperienced kicker, they rob him of power. This is because often half of the kick's energy is spent pushing his weight the rest of the way into position. This directs force into your body instead of into your opponent.

Second, improper weight transfer combined with a twisting action strains healthy knees and will blow bad knees. Focusing on ingraining weight transfer and balance before attempting to kick eases the strain on the joints. This significantly reduces the chances of long-term injury because students will no longer feel comfortable with or accept as normal the stress and strains of tornado kicking.

Third, by ingraining an awareness of balance, it will make learning different kinds of kicks faster and easier. Because all kicks require weight transfer, balance, and structure, this drill teaches you the alphabet before you try to read. It is a fundamental.

Once the student can consistently transfer weight and balance smoothly and efficiently, it is time to insert other details: establishing foot position, turning the foot in preparation for hip twists, timing the hip twist, and stepping into a kicking range. If these fundamental elements are not ingrained before the student tries to kick, they will be lost in the other details, and the student will default into tornado kicking.

Types of Kicks

For practical purposes, we are going to discuss how to kick from the front stance. By kicking from a stance, the student learns to feel the weight transfer from an 85 percent to 100 percent transition. During the weight transfer to kick in a stance, the student is taught to move smoothly without raising the body (by straightening the supporting knee). The stance puts the body lower to the ground and makes it feel much heavier, so the kick exercises the leg muscles and builds strength. The most common mistake is when students raise their bodies because their legs are not strong enough to absorb the necessary body weight transfer. Another benefit of training to kick from stances is that when you finally kick from a free fighting stance, it will feel easier and lighter.

Front Thrust Kick

The primary target is the solar plexus. The secondary target is the chin and throat area, using a high kick (high risk/high return).

Practice by transferring your weight and, at the same time, lift your knee as high as possible. Extend your leg slowly until the ball of your foot becomes the point of impact. Remember, the knee guides how high you kick (the knee is the "eye" of the leg).

This is the maximum force for your kick with normal energy use. After you've become comfortable practicing a slow motion front kick, then and only then should you attempt to kick forcefully with one motion. This means that when you finish the weight transfer, you also finish executing the front kick. Caution: make sure your leg is in full extension before you attempt to retreat or rechamber. A common mistake is pulling the leg back too early and before full extension. The full force of the kick is never delivered.

Front Upper Rising Kick or Groin Kick

The primary target is the groin. The secondary target is the chin, using a high kick (high risk/high return).

Practice by making a smooth weight transfer and simultaneously kicking the target with the instep of your foot without raising your knee. This is the *key* difference from the front thrust kick. Emphasize extending the kick to the fullest range before rechambering.

Side Thrust Kick

Lower side thrust kick: the primary target is the side of the knee or kneecap.

SIDE THRUST KICK

Correct: ready.   *Correct: transfer weight while covering centerline.*

Correct: twist and kick while still protecting centerline.

Practice by transferring 100 percent of your body weight onto one leg. At the same time, lift your knee as high as possible. The side of your ankle rests on the side of your supporting knee. Extend your leg slowly to the lower side until the side of your foot (knife edge) becomes the point of impact. After you've become comfortable practicing a slow-motion, lower side thrust kick, then and only then should you attempt to kick forcefully with one motion. This means that when you finish the weight transfer, you also finish executing the kick.

Caution: make sure your leg is in full extension before you attempt to retreat or rechamber. A common mistake is pulling the leg back too early before full extension. If this happens the full force of the kick is never delivered.

Middle side thrust kick: The primary target is the rib and solar plexus areas.

Practice by transferring 100 percent of your body weight on one leg. At the same time, lift your knee as high as possible. The side of your ankle rests on the side of your supporting knee. Extend your leg slowly to the side until the side of your foot (knife edge) becomes the point of impact. To maintain this, your kicking toe points down. After you've become comfortable practicing a slow-motion, middle side thrust kick, then and only then should you attempt to kick forcefully with one motion. This means that when you finish the weight transfer, you also finish executing the kick. Make sure your leg is in full extension before you attempt to retreat or rechamber. A common mistake is pulling the leg back too early and before full extension. The full force of the kick is never delivered.

Caution: do not lower your upper body (counterbalance) to offset any loss of balance. It will cost you if you do because your next move has to be bringing the upper body back to the center before you can do anything else. This is a crucial point in sparring or in any real situation.

Incorrect: Counterbalancing.

High side thrust kick: This kick has a very high risk of injury to whoever attempts it (very high risk/high return).

One hundred percent of your body weight will be on the nonkicking leg in a very stressful situation. Your body will be forced to bend to accommodate the high side thrust kick. You also might stress your muscles and possibly tear them.

It takes a lot of practice to have someone do the high-side thrust kick in slow motion. It can, however, look beautifully artistic and gymnastically acrobatic. If executed perfectly—meaning impeccable speed and timing, judgment of distance, and in the perfect environment that lends itself to the kick's usage—it will result in a high return. The target is hit with a full force that can knock a person out, or the very least stun him for a second of two.

Roundhouse Kick

The primary target is the side of the back knee area and solar plexus. The secondary target is the jaw (high risk). Practice by transferring 100 percent of your body weight to one leg. At the same time, raise the kicking leg with the knee bent. The leg is straightened to swing the foot into the target. The objective is to deliver a blow at a 90-degree angle, using the ball of the foot as the impact area. Feel the impact of your kick before rechambering.

Just like most high kicks, high roundhouses are high risk and high return.

ROUNDHOUSE KICK

Correct: ready.   *Correct: transfer weight.*

Correct: turn hips and kick.

A common problem with this kind of kick is moving only about 85 percent of your weight to the supporting leg and then launching it. The combination of the hip twist, the pivot of the supporting leg, and pushing off with the kicking leg creates a false spiraling effect that transfers the kicker's weight the rest of the way over his supporting leg. The kicking leg is already airborne at the time of weight transfer completion.

One often sees this kind of kick/weight transfer in point sparring. While it is arguably a faster way to kick, there is a significant drop in power. This is because a significant part of the force that should be available for power delivery into your opponent is now going into moving your weight that last 15 percent over your supporting leg.

KICK

Incorrect: ready.

Incorrect: twist, transfer weight and kick simultaneously.

Back Kick

Primary targets are the front and the side of the body. Use the heel of the foot as the primary point of impact. Step with your right foot crossing the left foot and turn 180 degrees. Raise your left knee and, using your right knee as your guide, deliver the kick. Be sure you fully extend the leg and that the toe is pointed down before you bring it back to a front stance.

BACK KICK

Correct: ready.

Correct: turn and transfer weight.

Correct: start kick.

Correct: finish kick.

~ 7 ~

Elbows

Importance of Proper Position

Before we bring the elbow strike into this discussion, we would like to reemphasize that positioning of the elbow is crucial. The elbow is the eye of the arm, the protector of the body, and the enforcer of most of the techniques found in the martial arts. As such, special attention must be paid to this important element.

Positioning the elbow is essential prior to executing an offensive technique (such as punching) or defensive movement (such as blocking) as well as in the guard position or fighting stance. Correct elbow position gives you the structure and posture you need to generate outgoing and handle incoming force. It also serves as the staging area to do any action easily and quickly.

Unfortunately, when doing a technique, many students focus on the furthest extent of the move (for example, the hand). By doing this they often create problems with their structure, but they don't realize what they are doing (leaning into a punch, locking elbows, bending wrists, putting the elbow in the wrong position, and so forth). These issues are often ignored when the individual is trying to compensate for a poor understanding of range by reaching out with the technique. Yes, the hand will still reach the target, but at the cost of structure and power. By shifting to teaching proper elbow placement and understanding range, many of these kinds of problems will evaporate because the student will no longer have to sacrifice proper posture to gain reach.

We will use the guard stance as a model to explain the importance of elbow position. The guard stance is left foot forward, weight equally distributed between both legs, left hand slightly bent, left fist level with the left eye, and the elbow approximately ten inches from the rib area. The right hand is slightly bent and the position is lower than the left hand.

Positioning your elbow too far from the body/rib area provides an opening for the would-be attacker. Position the elbow toward the floor to ensure a straight line for punches, but at the same time to protect the ribs.

ELBOWS

Correct.

Incorrect: elbows too high, chicken-winging.

Dropping Elbow against Attack

Kick coming in.

Drop elbow to protect side.

<u>DROPPING ELBOW AGAINST ATTACK</u> *(continued)*

Trap.

Lift and throw.

By lowering the elbow, one can easily protect the side of the body. If an upper block is required, merely raising the elbow up easily protects the face. You can use a lower block in a fighting stance where the fighter stands sideways to protect the groin area. The frontal area should be secured by the protection of the side or rib area. Proper positioning of the elbow will only give a little opening on the side. Therefore, if the attacker has launched the punch or kick to the rib region, you can just drop the elbow.

The side is protected and the only thing available to hit is bone (the hip, elbow), which hurts your attacker more than it does you. Proper elbow position requires a move of only a few centimeters to create a middle block, instead of the wild flailing that results from improper posture.

MIDDLE BLOCK

Correct: ready position.   *Correct: middle block.*

The correct posture puts your elbows in a position to only have to move inches, not feet. What's more, correct elbow position closes windows attacks can come through. The openings that are left open are much smaller and screened with a combination of movement (positioning) and the slightest flick of an elbow. Your blocking elbow covers your flank as you move away from the threat. It serves as a barrier, preventing the attack from following you.

For the record, let us state that the three main reasons people get hit are (1) not understanding range, (2) failing to move, and (3) bad elbow position. Each of these build on one another to let the attack get through. Students do not realize the attack does not start when the punch is in flight, it begins when the puncher steps into position to throw the strike (range). Recognizing this is how you get the time to move out of positioning for that attack. By failing to move, students augment their opponent's ability to exploit any windows in their defenses that they might have inadvertently left open. The only thing that can stop such an attack is the speed of your block. Finally, if your elbows are in the wrong position, you create windows that are too big to be effectively closed, no matter how fast you try—especially if you aren't moving away from the attack. Look at the advantage these factors create for your opponent: you don't know when the attack is coming, you can't move out of the way, you're wide open, and by the time you know it's coming, it's too late to stop it. No wonder his attacks get through.

With this in mind, take a closer look at the example of incorrect elbow positioning. To cover the head from all manner of attack, a person leaves himself exposed from the jaw down (imagine an uppercut to the jaw). Centerline is wide open. If this weren't bad enough, there is a further complication. By adopting an elbow position that is functionally a stunted high block, the person leaves no possible elbow movement save inward to protect his body. If he were to attempt an inside block—without twisting his body—the distance would be too great to cover. His block couldn't move fast enough to keep him from getting hit. From that posture, any movement except retreating and twisting would more than likely suck the punch into him. His incorrect elbow position has not only left him exposed, but also limits his choices for effective movement. This is one of the bigger reasons why elbow position must be closely studied and its significance understood.

Incorrect ready stance.

Elbow strikes are very powerful and devastating; this is their greatest advantage. But the elbow strike has disadvantages, too: namely, shorter range and misconceptions of how to execute the strike.

Different Elbow Strikes

There are four different elbow strikes: (1) forward upper rising elbow strike; (2) side elbow strike; (3) downward elbow strike; and (4) back elbow strike.

Forward Upper Rising Elbow Strike (Vertical Elbow)

The primary target is the chin and the side of the head.

VERTICAL ELBOW

Correct: ready.   *Correct: vertical elbow strike.*

This elbow doesn't come straight out from the shoulder, neither does it cross all the way over to centerline. In practice you should work at shooting it into a posture that is midway between the two.

If it comes straight out, not only are you left wide open for a counterattack along centerline (wrong posture), but you must be in a specific spot to hit your opponent in the chin. This spot is the farthest extreme of offensive distance (1 o'clock) or safe distance (11 o'clock). We say extreme because you are almost out of elbow range and back into punching range.

Incorrect: elbow straight out,
elbow not close to centerline.

Taking your elbow all the way over to centerline can be used as a defensive shielding move, without a supporting hand, but it can be structurally weak and unable to deliver or take force without collapsing. Also, like a straight-out elbow, it requires specific positioning, usually arising from flawed placement.

A posture that puts your elbow in between these two extremes is preferable. Not only are you still structurally strong, but the slight angle allows for ease of deflection. What is more important is that the angle of your upper arm lies along the angle your body moves to create proper distance. This brings an alignment of movement and structure that allows you to deliver maximum force.

Once you have the correct posture, practice throwing the elbow while moving into correct distance. When you move onto doing this on a heavy bag, you will find that this "middle" position combined with placement allows for more power delivery with less strain on your shoulder joint.

A slight straightening of the knees to increase the rising action of this blow can be added when you have perfected the placement of throwing this kind of elbow.

Side Elbow Strike (Horizontal Elbow)

The primary target is the side of the face or front of the face. The ribs can be targeted, as well.

You should be able to execute this technique without withdrawing your elbow back to the chambered position, but

SIDE ELBOW STRIKE

Correct: ready.

Correct: horizontal elbow, then return to ready position.

sequentially from any previous movement. From whatever you are doing, you can just fold your arm and throw this elbow—without cocking back and adding unnecessary movement. Since the elbow is a short-range weapon, you only waste precious time by chambering, time you cannot afford to lose with an opponent so close.

To be able to do this, you must understand that like a punch, a proper elbow comes from the hips and shoulders. A punch or a block can literally turn into an elbow strike with a flick of the hips.

This type of elbow strike is like a whip crack, your hips and shoulder movement not only sends it out, but also pulls it back. A boxing coach once described a punch in the following manner: Your hips are the cannon, your fist the cannonball. Your hips shoot the cannonball outward, while your arms are the ropes that pull the cannonball back. This is a good analogy, but it will not really work until you understand structure, posture, positioning, and placement. The exact same thing can be said about an elbow being a whip crack. You must have a solid understanding of structure and posture to correctly throw an elbow in this manner.

The reason is simple. If you are not in the correct posture, you will not relax. Your muscles lock down to hold you in the incorrect posture. Prematurely tightened muscles destroy effective power transfer.

Imagine a large bullwhip. Your hips are the whip's handle, your torso and shoulders are the thick part of the whip coming out of the handle. Although thick, this part is flexible and an integral part to transfer the movement of the handle to the whip's tip. As the handle moves, the thick part first flexes and then is dragged along. It is this combination of flexing and being dragged along that creates a wave of energy that will travel down the length of the whip. It takes the linear motion of how the handle is being moved that channels it into a wave.

If you allow yourself to relax, your body will naturally want to return to a structured pose. This fact is critical to understanding how to generate force through a wave motion. Your hips start the move, and your torso is pulled into the process. As the tension/pull increases, your shoulders, which until now haven't moved, will also be drawn into motion. If you were to do nothing else, your shoulders would catch up to your hips.

Instead of trying to tighten your arm and shoulder to throw an elbow, think of the whip. Hold your arm as though you were holding a small coin in the crook of your elbow, only keep enough pressure there to trap the coin. That is the only tension and it is the source of structure for the elbow strike. Imagine putting a fishing weight at the end of a whip and then getting struck by it.

As you whip your hips it only takes a small flick of your arm to position your elbow on the level that you want it to be. Once it gets up there it is dragged along with everything else. But wait until your hips have started to drag your shoulder before you pop your elbow up to where you want it to be. Otherwise you will have to tighten your shoulder to keep your elbow up there while waiting for the wave to work its way up your body. A tight shoulder will destroy the whip-crack effect.

Downward Elbow Strike

The primary target is the front or the back of the neck and head.

This is a secondary technique, meaning that it only can be applied if a target was presented as a response to a previous strike, or when the opportunity arises. The person must be in a bent-over position, which is why this move is often difficult to justify.

The downward elbow strike is not a move that you do except in extreme circumstances—that is to say, that the circumstances are bordering on life threatening or grave bodily injury. This move can and will cause serious damage, and should not be used without justifiable legal cause.

Like any other elbow strike, this move must have your body weight behind it for it to be effective. The move is combined with a weight drop. You start with a knee bend to get your weight moving in a downward direction; near the end of the weight drop you strike with your elbow. Without this timing and weight drop, the move loses its efficiency.

WEIGHT DROP/ELBOW STRIKE

Correct: ready position.   *Correct: downward elbow.*

Back Elbow Strike

This elbow strike is designed to hit the target behind you. Therefore, it is useful if you have been grabbed from behind.

The back elbow strike is inherent in many hard-style katas. When the fist is withdrawn to the hip, you have just performed the arm action. It is here that the efforts you have put into hip/shoulder twists will pay off. This elbow strike is generated from the hips, not the shoulders. A firm understanding of push/pull power generation—a foundation of kata—will also greatly assist you in developing this move's power.

An elbow strike is a short-range weapon. It is the strongest of all strikes, but it must be done in the right range. Do not attempt to overreach with this technique. Wait until either your opponent is in range or you have moved into the correct range. Any of these techniques will suffer if you lean in an attempt to gain extra reach.

Another important part of elbow strikes is to keep the angle of the elbow consistent.

BACK ELBOW STRIKE

Correct: ready position.   *Correct: back elbow strike.*

~ 8 ~

Takedowns and Throws

Difference between a Takedown and a Throw

There is a big difference between a takedown and a throw. Understanding this difference is instrumental in performing both effectively.

We have already discussed structure as putting your skeleton in the proper posture to deliver the force of your body movement. In a more common definition, structure is what allows you to stand upright and walk. Your bones are taking most of the weight. The little muscle you use keeps you standing and in balance. Base is how that structure is connected to the earth—preferably giving your structure stability and balance. Balance is the ongoing process of aligning your structure and base so you can remain upright.

Both takedowns and throws rely on affecting your opponent's structure, base, and balance.

A takedown technique is disrupting a person's structure/balance and then preventing his reestablishing a base. Once that happens, he falls. It is the martial arts equivalent of catching your foot in a crack in the sidewalk and not being able to get it out in time to save yourself from falling. When you do a takedown, you are the crack your opponent trips over.

<u>Takedown</u>

Block, enter, placing foot.

Takedown over placed foot.

Gravity is the main force. Other smaller amounts of force are used to put your opponent into the grip of gravity. Takedowns are usually based on subtle movements. Their success depends on establishing a counter to the person's attempts to regain balance or reestablish structure. Once your opponent's balance is destroyed, you don't let him get a foot out to save himself, nor do you let him grab onto anything. This can be done in either one or sequential moves.

We would like to emphasize that the eight directional clock points are important parts of throws or takedowns. Each point may be used to disrupt your opponent's normal balance, provided the technique is executed correctly. For example, have a student standing firmly with both feet on the ground and facing 9 o'clock. His right foot is at 12 o'clock and left foot at 6 o'clock. Now place your palm between his shoulder blades. A slight push or pull from 3 o'clock will easily unbalance him. However, his balance will be naturally strong along the 6 o'clock and 12 o'clock axis. To disrupt that balance change the direction of the pull and push toward the remaining six directional points. Students who are leaning how to do throws or takedowns must understand the directional principles.

Nature of Throws

A throw involves force beyond gravity that overwhelms the person's base and structure and hurls him. There is so much force and motion involved that the person is catapulted beyond any chance of recovery. Throws are usually multistep processes requiring several different types of movement.

Throws come in two basic forms: voluntary and involuntary. A voluntary throw is where, in response to a joint lock or other pain-inducing move, the person throws himself. He does this to protect himself from pain or to prevent something from being sprained or broken. You supply the motivation; he supplies the movement or energy.

An involuntary throw is where you literally pick up the person and hurl him. You either disrupt his structure or uproot his balance, then you catapult him. Through external force, you destroy his structure and prevent him from reestablishing it or base. It doesn't matter if he wants to be thrown or not. You supply the leverage, energy, and motivation; he goes along for the ride.

There is a great deal of overlap in these definitions. A sweep of the supporting leg is an example of a large dynamic force used against structure in a way that prevents the opponent from reestablishing his base. So although it is a takedown, it is not subtle. On the other hand, small circle jujitsu is based on a small, subtle move that results in the person throwing himself. By definition, however, as refined as it is, it is still a throw.

Destroying versus Disrupting Structure

Before we go on, we would like to address an important misconception. A very common mistake by many students who attempt to execute a throw is that they are unaware of the distinction between destroying and disrupting someone's structure.

Destroying connotes breaking or annihilating something. In approaching the idea of takedowns and throws, many students feel they must utterly destroy someone's structure. Picking someone up and hurling him is an example of destroying structure and base, as is hitting someone so hard that you knock him down.

VOLUNTARY THROW

Block.

Counter strike, disrupting his structure.

<u>VOLUNTARY THROW</u> *(continued)*

Figure four lock.

Attacker throws himself to avoid pain.

INVOLUNTARY THROW

Block, strike, and move into position.

Disrupt attacker's structure.

<u>Involuntary Throw</u> *(continued)*

Begin throw.

Finish throw.

It is possible to effectively destroy someone's structure without leaving yourself exposed, but that is not how it usually happens. Most people tend to overdo their efforts. Since they don't know how to effectively destroy structure, they try to make it up through sheer volume of force. This is overkill.

Instead, they generally lose any and all subtlety and, by extension, flow. They act as though they are trying to break bones, instead of collapsing structure. Instead of making their efforts a single, GPS–guided missile to take out a building, they try for a 50-kiloton nuke to flatten the entire city. Unfortunately, in trying to generate all this force, they so overcommit that they destroy their posture, leave themselves exposed, and fail to achieve positioning.

DESTROYING

Incoming blow.

<u>DESTROYING</u> *(continued)*

Block.

Destroy structure.

By trying so hard to destroy their opponent's structure, they are not in a position to do anything if they fail—and fail they often do.

Disrupting is far more subtle and achieves the same end of putting your opponent into the grip of gravity or teetering on the edge of a fall—but without the overkill and risk. When your opponent's balance or structure is disrupted, he is left in a precarious position. He must address the immediate problem of gravity or fall. He cannot effectively counterattack because any motion not oriented toward reestablishing a base will result in a fall.

Yes, disruption can be achieved by breaking something. But you can accomplish the same objective with subtlety (for example, instead of trying to bowl an opponent over, you push your knee into the back of his while pulling down on his shoulder). Subtlety is important because you stay in a better position for your next move. And, yes, your next move is that little shove or pull that puts him over the cliff's edge.

The directional movements to disrupt an opponent's balance must be executed in a smooth manner, without pauses or jerks. Sometimes an opponent will resist efforts to offset his balance, therefore, the defender must move smoothly and in one continuous motion, in any direction, to keep his opponent constantly off balance until a proper technique can be applied.

Fundamentals of Both

Throws and takedowns share a great many similarities. They both work better through leverage than muscle. Leverage is a far greater force than muscle alone. To achieve leverage, you must remember to move correctly along the proper angles.

(Proper angles cannot be explained effectively in a book. They must be demonstrated to and practiced by the student.)

How do you test for correct angles? If it feels easy, you are moving correctly.

It is not hard work to move someone down the correct angle. This exploits inherent weaknesses in your opponent's structure. The human body easily twists, folds, and unbalances in certain ways. A correct angle is hard to resist. It is, however, hard work to move someone down the incorrect angle because you are fighting structural design. The body naturally resists force in that direction. Moving someone down the wrong angle requires muscle and hard work because he can fight you.

What we can also tell you is that 99 percent of the problem of finding the right angle arises from your being in the wrong position. That puts you in the wrong range and makes finding the correct angle almost impossible. Both range and position must be practiced: study moving into both. Practice it over and over until you can easily slide where you need to be. Don't worry about completing the throw or takedown yet. Just get to where you can nearly always step into both the right range and position and disrupt an opponent's structure.

A common example of bad positioning is when you find that you cannot take the correct angle because you are standing where you need to move your opponent. Another example is when you cannot move your body far enough to generate sufficient force for a throw. So is being in a place where you cannot prevent your opponent from reestablishing his base: you pushed him, but you couldn't stop him from getting his foot out to save himself.

Another commonality that throws and takedowns share is that both must be "set up" before being executed. You must not only be in position, but you must disrupt your opponent's structure. This means placement. It's not just moving into position, it's also disrupting his structure as you move.

Throws are more powerful, but they cost more. They take more time and effort than takedowns. You pay for the extra damage of a throw with the time and difficulty to set it up. Sometimes, however, an attacker makes a present of himself by moving into a position from which you can capitalize. This is another reason why deflection is strategically important. When you deflect rather than stopping your opponent's momentum, you now have the opportunity to redirect the opponent's motion. Involuntary throws are powerful, but they take more time and energy to perform effortlessly than other techniques, such as strikes, elbows, and takedowns.

Remember this fundamental difference: one is based on all that you must do to create placement so you can throw; the other is based on what you must keep your opponent from doing to save himself from falling.

Takedowns rely on an incontestable force of nature—gravity. Once your opponent's base is gone, he's going down. With takedowns, you must simply disrupt his structure and prevent him from reestablishing a solid base.

Throws, if they are not developed properly, can be contested on many fronts (for example, size, strength, ability to resist pain, and so forth). With throws, you must first disrupt and then overwhelm your opponent's structure and base. The trick is to do this second part before he can counter the first. If you are not in control of the first part, then that will indeed be tricky.

It's important to note that involuntary throws have a very limited range. They must be done very close in. Takedowns, however, can be done up to kicking distance (for example, sweeps). To do a throw, you must enter the correct range.

<u>THROWS</u>

Block.

Disrupt structure.

Strike and position.

Throw.

Let's move on to a more concrete and demonstrable problem. Although based in theory and principle, it is an error that is very easy to identify and demonstrate.

In perfecting both takedowns and throws, the martial arts fundamental of *weakness prevailing against strength* is paramount. Nowhere else is it so blatantly obvious when someone violates this principle by applying too much muscle. You can see him take a stance and strain as he hurls the person. What makes this approach difficult to argue is its success rate. A larger and stronger person can literally pick up and hurl a smaller, weaker opponent most of the time. The inherent weakness of this approach, however, is revealed when contesting with an opponent of equal or greater strength. Putting it bluntly, as long as you pick on little guys, this strategy works.

Or will it?

Strength works against a smaller opponent when the smaller person is unfamiliar with the criteria of throws and takedowns. The smaller person, therefore, allows the larger person to establish his base and use muscle. Then the smaller person attempts to contest with the same. At this point, the larger person has the conditions he needs for his size and strength to prevail. The smaller person is now playing the larger person's game and is almost guaranteed to lose.

Basically, the same elements that make an effective throw also serve as the means to prevent you from being thrown by brute force. By using them, you do not allow the stronger person to create the conditions he needs to throw you with strength.

Strength is built on the foundation of structure and base. Without those two elements, strength won't work. The strongest man on this planet is helpless if he is floating in space because he has no base to push or pull from. Understanding this point is critical for both throwing and not being thrown. Through positioning and placement, you don't allow him the structure or base that he needs. That is one way weakness overcomes strength.

Certain fundamental criteria are inherent to either a throw or takedown. These are: moving, affecting structure, countering, using leverage, changing direction, and changing level. While each of these are critical components, what brings them together and blends them into a unified whole is flowing motion. It is flowing motion that creates the dynamic results that far outstrip the individual parts.

Flowing motion takes these fundamentals, mixes them, and gives them the shake that results in explosive power.

It should be the goal of any practitioner of these arts to become more subtle, regardless of whether he is doing throws or takedowns. The more subtle you are, the better your flow. You achieve more with less. You become an alchemist learning the subtle art of mixing these components and seeking perfection in blending them. The more subtle the mix, the less muscle and strength you use—and, like properly mixed nitroglycerin, the greater the explosion.

Movement

Movement is what gives you power. Momentum is created by moving your weight with speed and in a particular direction. Any time you stop moving, you will be forced to try to complete the technique with muscle. This is why we say we can tell when someone uses muscle. In the middle of the technique, the person will literally stop moving, bend his knees and then straighten up. He will then continue to move to finish the technique.

Affecting Structure

We have already gone on extensively about affecting structure. But we'd like to take a closer look at why many throws fail. A disruption is to a throw what blasting caps are to dynamite. You first create a small explosion that creates what is necessary for the bigger one. Without the blasting cap, the dynamite won't go off. The disruption sets up the destruction.

A fundamental problem is when people are so focused on destruction that they don't realize that they have created disruption. Not recognizing it, they can't exploit it to attain the destruction they were aiming for.

Destroying someone's structure is not easy, but most people make it more difficult by trying too hard. That is why they overshoot disruption. A failed destruction will still result in a disruption. But because the person was trying so hard, he will be in neither the posture nor the position to exploit it and do a takedown or complete the throw.

There are many metaphors that can be used to show this idea. One is that there is a high school boy who has two girls in his life. The first is the more attractive, popular homecoming queen, but she can be fickle and unreliable. The second girl is not as pretty as the homecoming queen, but is both cute and intelligent. What's more, she is also far more reliable, level-headed, and she likes the boy. But the boy, being blinded by his pursuit of the homecoming queen, spurns the second girl. (Who was, by far, the better choice to have a stable, long-term relationship with rather than the elusive homecoming queen.) In the end, he has neither.

Often young and inexperienced fighters ignore the more reliable disruption and try to charge in for the destruction. Like the story, they end up with neither. Unlike the dating metaphor, however, the results of this failure are disastrous . . . unless you end the story with the spurned girl returning to brain him with a cast-iron frying pan—which is analogous to what happens when you fail to disrupt or destroy an opponent's structure. Not only have you failed, but you've put yourself in the wrong position to be in with someone who wants to hurt you.

Compare that, however, to the following set of photos. In the first, the thrower disrupts the person's structure, offbalancing him. Then he simply counters the uke's attempt to reestablish structure. Without his structure beneath him, the uke must fall. This fall is not negotiable; the law of gravity guarantees it.

The thrower manages to destroy the uke's structure and then uses leverage to throw him. At no time did the defender sacrifice his own structure, position, or placement to achieve that destruction.

If while trying to destroy your opponent's structure, you sacrifice what you need to complete the move properly, the only option left is to attempt to complete the throw through muscle. This is a patch job, and it is very likely to fail. While you are trying to get structure back, so is your opponent.

Countering

Countering reestablishment of structure is largely dependent on understanding the three nearly instinctual reactions to loss of balance. By nearly instinctive we mean that as human beings, we have been walking so long that we have ingrained certain responses to the point that they are unconscious reactions.

Any unconscious reaction to reestablish base is going to be faster than a rattlesnake strike. A person may step or pivot to

ATTEMPTED DISRUPT

Incoming blow.

Block and positioning.

170

Disrupt structure.

Throw.

stay on his feet. If you are behind the ball on countering this, your chances of catching up, much less preventing it, are slim to none. This is why you must plan for, and take prior steps, to prevent these reactions.

Reaction No. 1—*Step and attempt to reestablish base underneath one's structure.*

This is exactly what stumbling is. It is hurriedly trying to get a base under your structure and weight before you fall. What few people realize is that this action is as instinctive as walking, because it *is* walking. The process of walking and running is one where you transfer your weight forward and reestablish new bases under your structure in its new position. It is a natural reaction, and it is exactly what foils most throw and takedown attempts.

The next time you observe takedowns or throws, watch for the opponent stepping and reestablishing base. The times he does will overwhelmingly turn into wrestling matches.

It is also instinctive for people to put their hands out in an attempt to create a counterbalance to compensate for the shaky base they may have temporarily established. This counterbalance doesn't slow the actual fall. Once you start falling, gravity dictates the speed. What putting your hands out can do is keep you teetering on the edge of falling, thereby allowing you to get a foot out and establish a stronger base. The arms going out lead to reaction No. 2.

Reaction No. 2—*Grab onto something.*

This reaction is embedded in the process that leads from getting your arms out to counterbalance and Reaction

No. 3, which is why it is so often not noticed. It is part two of a three-stage process.

This is an attempt to gain extra base by grabbing onto something more solid. Flailing hands grab onto things. Flailing arms wrap around and hug the closest thing to prevent falling. In this case, that means you. If you have ever attempted to do a throw and ended up going down with your opponent, that is what happened. He grabbed and took you down with him.

To prevent a person from countering your attempts at throws or takedowns, you must disrupt his structure and control both his torso (to prevent him from grabbing you) and his legs and feet (to prevent him from stepping and reestablishing base). Failure to do either of these means there will be a good chance you will have a fight on your hands.

Reaction No. 3—*Put your hands out to soften the fall.*

This is often mistakenly called "catching yourself." That doesn't happen. Your arms serve as shock absorbers to soften the impact of your fall. They don't stop it. What this action does is keep you from knocking your teeth out or splitting your skull.

You want to prevent the first two reactions. The third, however, is a matter of choice. How hard you want to put the person down determines if you want to prevent it or not. Generally if you don't want to hurt someone, you release his arms in time to let him soften his landing—but only after he is past where he can grab you to save himself.

The process of takedown can be summed up as: break his balance and prevent him from reestablishing it. The latter is much easier if you know these three instinctive reactions and have a plan to counter them before you break his balance. The same process is present with throws, except there is an additional step at the end.

Leverage

Leverage is perhaps the most commonly used word in regard to the throwing arts. At the same time, it is probably the most poorly understood. Most people who think they are using leverage correctly are actually using muscle—and the wrong kind of leverage.

Leverage is a mechanical force arising from specific conditions you create. It is the type of force you can only generate when everything is in its correct place.

There are four elements to leverage: (1) fulcrum, (2) load, (3) effort, and (4) lever. Imagine two children on a teeter-totter. The bar the teeter-totter rocks on is the fulcrum. When one child is down near the ground, his weight is the load (that which needs to be moved). The force of the other child's descending weight is the effort. The teeter-totter (that both children are sitting on) is the lever. This is the formula for the different types of leverage. A throw will go wrong if you have not established these necessary components in your technique.

There are three types of levers. A first-class lever is where the fulcrum is between the load and the effort. This is how a majority of throws operate. Your opponent is the load, your body is the fulcrum, and your movement is the effort. You lever him over your hips or shoulder. This principle also works with voluntary throws, except that one of his own joints becomes the fulcrum. The small twist you apply is the effort; his body is the load that is moved.

FIRST-CLASS LEVER

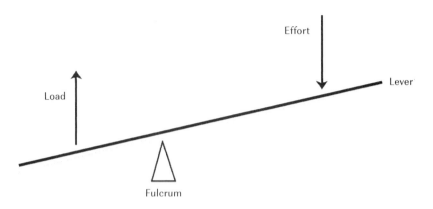

A second-class lever has the same elements, but they are arranged differently. The fulcrum is at the end. The load is located between the fulcrum and the effort—on top of the lever. The best example of this is a wheelbarrow. When you lift the handle, the load is lifted up easier because of the fulcrum at the other end. This kind of leverage is used extensively in one way to disrupt someone's structure. The person's foot serves as the fulcrum. His body weight is the load. Instead of shoving straight, you push more in an upward and forward direction (as you would a wheelbarrow) toward his foot. This shifts the load toward the fulcrum. To stay upright, the person must either bring his structure back into alignment over this base (rare) or step out with the other foot. This is an act you don't allow. Second-class levers also are used in takedowns when you shift the load over the fulcrum and then knock it out from under him. You sweep the supporting leg you created by levering his weight onto it.

It's when we come to the third-class lever that things go horribly wrong with the way most people try to use leverage in

SECOND-CLASS LEVER

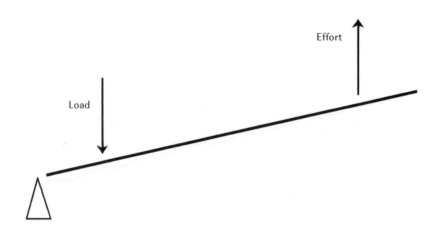

the throwing arts. In a third-class lever, the fulcrum is at one end, the load is at the other, and the effort is between. Swinging a baseball bat is a perfect example of a third-class lever. The batter's body is the fulcrum. His twisting movement is the effort. The load is the weight of the bat meeting the resistance of the ball's momentum.

Using leverage this way is great when you are swinging a kali stick or throwing muay Thai kicks, but it is horrible when you are trying to do a throw from the wrong position.

That is exactly what most people try to do when they use muscle. They step forward and take a rooted stance (fulcrum), reach out and grab the person (load), and then try to hurl him (effort). They make themselves the lever. This takes a lot of effort. It is the way people are taught to hit with sticks and kicks and is how they try to use third-class levers in throws and takedowns.

THIRD-CLASS LEVER

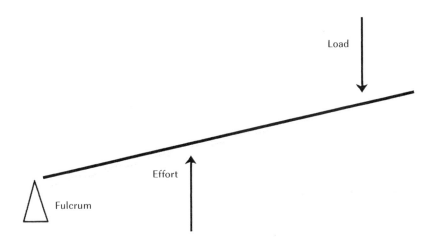

Load

Effort

Fulcrum

You do use third-class levers in takedowns, and you do it all the time. Another example of a third-class lever is to imagine a table with four legs. Now take two of those from one side. The fulcrum is the remaining two legs, the effort is gravity, and the load is the table's weight. That's how you use third-class levers in takedowns: you make your opponent the lever—*not* you. You take out a leg and prevent him from getting it back out in time to save himself.

When it comes to throwing, leverage is to muscle what Taiko drumming is to pounding two rocks together. While both are percussion, past that there is just no comparison. Once you are familiar with the difference between leverage and muscle, it will virtually scream at you. You will immediately feel it and say to yourself, "No! Wrong!"

Being thrown by muscle is like being blown by a strong wind. You will feel it pressing against you. With leverage, it

LEVERAGE

Tristan using a third-class lever.

Uke being the third-class lever.

feels like "a whisper solidified." It's almost as though the earth suddenly falls away beneath your feet, and you find yourself flying through the air with no idea how you got there.

When you use muscle, you feel the drag and stress against your structure. You also will feel the pull and strain as your muscles try to compensate for your bad positioning and lack of leverage. When done correctly, both throws and takedowns are no more stressful than walking.

Direction Changes

Direction changes are another criteria for effective throws and takedowns. These can come in two basic ways. One is circular motion. By its nature, a circular motion involves changing direction. If you take a circle and break it down into a series of straight lines, you can easily see these inherent directional changes. Just imagine a force running along the circumference in a clockwise manner.

This continual change in direction never allows your opponent to establish an effective base for resistance. When he establishes a base to resist a particular line of force, the line of force changes direction, and it's a direction that his newly established base can't resist. To save himself, he has to establish another base. The continuing directional changes eventually outrun his attempts to create base and structure.

Another way to change directions is just to put a move that is going one way into reverse along approximately the same line. A push becomes a pull, a pull becomes a push. Although we say reverse, these moves work better if you do not follow the exact line, and instead add a certain element of up or down to change levels on the original line.

A simple way to see both kinds of directional change can be done with a willing partner. Firmly grasp your uke's wrist and, with your body acting as a pivot, begin to pull him clockwise around you. To do this, you must spin your body and keep your arm locked. Pull in one direction until he manages to get one of his feet out far enough to resist. When he does, change direction and spin counterclockwise. Play with this simple exercise until you can continuously keep your partner dancing around you in circles.

There are many more ways that circular motion will affect both you and your opponent. Unfortunately, too many people attempt to grasp these deeper truths before they understand the implications and applications of directional change—especially when it comes to preventing the person you are throwing from resisting your action. This is like trying to read before you have learned the alphabet. The exercise we have just given you will greatly assist in learning the basics of directional change and when to do it.

Three things are important in any directional change. First, directional change always comes from body movement. You do not generate force through your arm muscles. It is your body that is moving one direction and suddenly, unexpectedly, moves in another.

Second, maintain contact. Usually this means grip. An open-hand push becomes a grab and then a pull. Although it can also mean a flip of the wrist that puts your hand on the other side, making your opponent susceptible to the changing direction of the force. Without this contact, it is much harder to control your opponent because you lose track of his location. Often contact is lost at the critical moment when the whiplash effect should be delivered into him.

Third, do not lose structure and, by extension, control. Do not allow your structure to fall apart when you want to change the directional force (i.e., go noodle-armed or allow your arms to hyperextend). It is important to keep your structure intact, especially during the stress and strain of the directional change. If you allow your arms to collapse or extend out, they act as giant rubber bands that stretch and flex instead of delivering your body's momentum into your opponent.

The most common mistakes people commit in directional changes can usually be traced to a failing in one of these three listed, and they may compound each other. A mistake in one can cause a mistake in the others. Without these three fundamentals firmly ingrained in your technique, things will go wrong. You will have no choice but to attempt to use muscle to complete the move.

The final point about directional change is sensitivity. There is a very simple rule about when to do it: when you feel resistance, it is time to change direction.

We don't mean the drag of his weight. If you feel too much of that, you are not in the right place, and you are not using leverage. Use a directional change when you feel him "pushing back" against your efforts.

If you have disrupted his structure and you feel resistance, he has somehow reestablished his base (usually by stepping). This does not mean that his base is necessarily a solid one. If you continue pushing in that direction, the only thing you will do is encourage him to take another step and establish a much stronger base. In short, if you attempt to overpower his resistance, you most often help him create a better base and structure to resist you further.

By changing direction, you force him to abandon that attempt at a base and try to create a new one to prevent falling.

A directional change, in essence, says, "Oh, you've got base in that direction? That's OK because you don't have it in this one." As your opponent is in effect stumbling to stay upright anyway, this added challenge often proves too much. He can't get his foot out to where it needs to be to save himself.

This is especially true if you just so happen to put your foot out to trip him. There is no reason—with a little practice—you cannot do direction changes so the new path leads right over your front foot.

Level Changes

Level changes are the final criteria for effective throws or take-downs. These techniques are almost never done on the horizontal plane. They are performed on diagonal, circular, and spiral planes. These moves are not parallel to the ground, rather they head toward it—maybe not in the first part of the move, but they always end up heading that way.

Most people fail to achieve level changes because they do not occur out in the front lines—where their hands are engaging their opponent and all their attention is focused—but in the rear—away from all the action. Level changes take place at the knees.

It is by bending and straightening the knees in conjunction with other types of body movement that creates directional movement along these planes. A hip turn combined with bending your rear leg creates a downward spiral. A simple forward weight transfer combined with bending your front knee creates a diagonal, downward drive. This also applies to voluntary takedowns. A small circular twist of his wrist causes your opponent's knees to buckle.

Since we normally walk without too much change in levels, we tend to be able to easily resist forces along horizontal lines. If pushed or pulled, we just move to a new position on the horizontal plane. Our skeletons allow us to strongly resist vertical pressure. By blending both horizontal and vertical movement, we get diagonal movement, and that movement is a multidirectional force.

A multidirectional force—one that changes our position not only on the horizontal plane but also on the vertical—tends to be too much to easily handle. We have the means to cope with one or the other, but not both at once.

Unfortunately, many people who attempt throws fail to ensure that these important criteria are present in their techniques. These elements are the cornerstones to effective and effortless throws and takedowns. You must practice them individually to understand them and ingrain them into your priorities and reactions. By studying them individually as component parts, you will begin to see their importance.

Critical Components

You do not learn these cornerstone elements by osmosis. Knowing a complete technique does not mean you automatically master, much less ingrain, these skills that make the move work. By practicing them individually until they are automatically present in your technique, you will ensure their presence under stress. Your body will react exactly the way it is trained. If your training hasn't ensured the presence of these elements, they won't be there when you need them.

Without these fundamentals, you will not be able to throw effectively, and you greatly increase the likelihood of being thrown yourself. These elements not only make your throws better, but they give you an understanding of what your opponent needs to effectively throw you. You also will know how to prevent him from using these components.

There are many other important aspects that we could have mentioned about throws and takedowns. What we have addressed here are the most common mistakes, misunderstandings, and omissions. This is a checklist. Take what we have presented, run troublesome techniques by these criteria, and see if everything we've discussed is there. Often you will find parts missing and will be able to put them back in.

— 9 —

Traditional Asian Weapons

Martial arts weapons have gained popularity in the West through depictions of their use in movies and later from Asian martial artists who traveled to the United States and Europe. Western audiences were wowed by flashy displays of both traditional military weapons and the exciting idea of exotic improvised weapons.

One thing that many students of the weapons arts fail to understand is that weapons and fighting arts are a legitimate and prominent part of all Asian cultures. But there are too many gaps between the myths and the facts to completely understand the use of any specific weapon.

We make this statement based upon the observation that Western "understanding" of Eastern weapons is a weird blend of myth, fantasy, half-truths, a lack of knowledge about history, misunderstandings of cultural and societal norms, and misunderstanding of what is involved in weapon use, application, effects, and limitations. What is most evident however is a lack of knowledge about the changes in the items themselves.

Myths of Weapons

Western martial arts students do not understand that most of what they consider traditional weapons—nunchaku (nunchucks), bos, three-section staffs, tonfas, sticks, and so forth—aren't the agrarian tools that legend makes them out to be. It's not that they weren't originally, but what is sold in martial arts supply stores are modified versions, designed and weighted for demonstration and modern martial arts display. Their weight and design are for fast, flashy display, not for application in combat. As such they are neither agrarian tools, military weapons, nor realistic personal weapons.

Although myths of these items being used to fight samurai abound, in their original form they were not weapons. Most were everyday farming and fishing tools. If they were used as improvised weapons it was for stopgap personal defense, not something you would consistently rely on or carry into battle. They definitely are not something that you used to try fighting an armed and trained samurai.

Other items such as the sai and the manriki gusari are not farm implements at all. They were imported from other countries and used by law enforcement officers. A persistent myth, for example, reinforced by movies, is that the sai was used for disarming a sword-wielding opponent. They were, in fact, primarily used as truncheons by what we would consider law enforcement officers. These weapons were employed as part of a larger, more coordinated defensive tactics strategy involving several men with various weapons. Although a sai works against both smaller and improvised weapons, you would not want to go against a swordsman with one.

Often people invent creative uses for these and improvised weapons, asserting, "This is how it was used." They usually fail to take into account centuries of history, cultural forces, social standing within cultures, political upheaval, military advancement, and technological change. The disarming of samurai, for example, only occurred during the very few years of the Meiji Restoration; prior to that an attack on a samurai would be an unthinkable crime.

Yet blanket claims about Oriental weapons use are accepted at face value by students when the "master" speaks. Or is he just parroting what he has heard? What's more, masters making these claims have no idea how many of these mythologies about the martial arts were created by nationalistic/political spinmeisters in the last century. An independent study—and by this we mean using historical rather than martial arts sources— of the prewar Japanese propaganda efforts and the post–Korean War politics regarding the development of a national sport is an eye-opening endeavor.

In general we believe what we are told by our teacher, regardless of what types of weapons are used. This is why we say there are too many gaps between the myths and the facts to completely understand the use of any specific weapon. How can someone know how an improvised weapon was used to defeat a sword if that person has no real knowledge of how a sword is used—much less how a sword is used in different schools of "fencing"? Has he ever tried to use this item to disarm an attacking, uncooperative swordsman?

Having said this, however, we do encourage the study of weapons. Not as means of self-defense or becoming steeped in the warrior arts, but because of the discipline, concentration, physical skill, and lessons in tradition, ceremony, and ritual.

With this in mind we would like to give you some pointers that will have an effect on your approach to learning weapons.

Purposes of Weapons and Weapons Training

The first objective of any weapon is to gain distance. This means that its use should give you the ability to reach your opponent before he reaches you. It also can create a safe distance where the opponent is within your reach, but can't reach you or will have difficulty reaching you. The longer the weapon's reach, the more objectives it can attain. It does not mean a victory, it just means more advantage in gaining a potential victory.

Much of the history of warfare is based on this simple principle. Gaining distance is the reason we have modernized fighting weapons. In early times, warriors used arrows as their artillery, then eventually changed to cannons. Today, we are more sophisticated, that is, smart bombs, missiles, and so forth. Yet the objectives are still the same: gain safe distance or hit the target from a safe distance.

In hand-to-hand combat where each combatant has traditional weapons, each will try to use his weapon to gain distance and advantage. Combined with skill, will, and luck, one of them can walk away victorious. Traditional weapons began with knives, swords, long bo, long staff with two feet of knife on top of it, and so forth, and eventually evolved to handguns, rifles, and assault rifles. Again, all methods were designed to use a weapon to gain safe distance and the advantage.

Many modern masters craft or develop new weapons for self-defense in the West. However, they fail to understand the importance of distance. They often demonstrate the use of their weapons with the assumption that their opponents will be remaining in place to receive the blow or will actually cooperate. Remember, by definition, your opponent is not on your side: he will not be cooperating. Odds are he will be launching his own offense, an offense that can be just as devastating as yours.

In light of this: if you are using a weapon, but are not gaining any distance or reach, it's a risky proposition.

Every time you commit both hands to holding the weapon, the freedom of your hand movements is disrupted. The question then becomes why tie up your hands by use of a weapon if there is no advantage of reach? One common answer is: so I can hit as hard as I can without hurting my hand.

There's a simple answer to that contention. If your opponent hits you first, you will be on the ground and not all the techniques in the world will help you. If you are holding a weapon that only gives you one or two inches of advantage and is a blunt object, such as a short stick, your task to gain your objectives becomes harder, not easier.

About the only technique you can use without dropping your weapons is usually a hammer fist. That hammer fist is good for a second or the third technique, but it doesn't generally work if it is the first technique used. To use the hammer fist, either forward or back, is too risky. It has a longer path to travel to impact, opens you too wide, and is not practical. You can use a hammer fist in conjunction with the straight punch or backfist . . . but why? Why use the stick at all?

Simply stated, such items are best used against an unwilling opponent. They have a very strong surprise factor in that they do cause a disproportionate amount of pain. In other words, that blow should not have hurt that much. This surprise factor will often cause a person, who is more emotional than committed to combat, to shy away from the intensity of the pain. If someone is prone to run away at the first sign of resistance, then this tool works well. Unfortunately, by the very definition of facing an unwilling opponent, the use of a weapon is not legally justified.

But if the person is truly committed to harming you, then all the problems we have discussed are manifest. The extra pain you cause is not sufficient compensation for the loss of hand mobility.

Using a sharp object, such as a knife, can be more practical and effective, even with only one or two inches of distance gained. With sharp objects, movement can be fluid and deadly. But most of all, the weapon will psychologically affect the potential attacker.

The old saying that "the weapon is an extension of the hands" is true. But the bottom line is that without the courage or determination to use the weapon, a high degree of skill is useless. It is like having a great painting of Picasso, then storing it away in the closet where no one can see it.

In the old days, before the development of firearms, traditional weapons were very effective in battle. Weapons and fighting arts were life itself. By its very nature, Asian martial arts is highly ritualized, moderately paced, and can be so obvious—yet have hidden applications. In this modern day, the higher purpose of learning martial arts is to develop the mind and spirit of the warrior. This is not an easy path. It takes years of daily training to cultivate these attributes. There can be no thorough understanding of Asian martial arts without a substantial understanding of its combatives.

This is not to say that learning traditional weapons is not beneficial, rather this book will guide you to achieving your goal of learning the traditional weapon.

But it is highly unlikely that you will ever slip into traditional customs, sling your sword on your back, walk down the street, and prepare to use your skills to defend yourself or take your own justice in the 'hoods, like a warrior in the movies.

So what is the benefit of learning the Asian traditional weapons? First, you have to define your goals. Are you learning the weapons solely for the love of the art? For the discipline involved or required in all Asian martial arts? For self-defense? Or solely for a fighting skill to harm or to kill another human being? Your answer should be the first option—love of the art. If your objective is to kill people, you can purchase a gun and go to the shooting range. With a good instructor, you can learn to shoot effectively in a very short time, rather than investing in years of training.

So before you commit to the study of traditional Asian weapon arts, you have to have a goal, and your training goal must be worthwhile.

"You should train to become like this boulder, with most of your strength hidden and so deeply rooted that you are immovable. Yet so powerful that what can be seen will make men cringe to walk in your shadow," master Japanese swordsman Musashi told his disciple as they passed under the boulder that loomed above their path.

The myths of weapons are that they give you more power. But what is power? First you must know the limitations and range. Second, power is a device. There is no positive or negative value to it. Its success can be measured only through its achievement, and it depends on how you measure the accomplishment. Power can be as much to your advantage as to your disadvantage. Last, some people think power is everything. The truth is power is always less effective than its processor estimates it to be.

It's true a weapon can save your life, but it can also put you in prison for life if misused. The decision to use a weapon will be yours. The decision if that use was justified or misused belongs to others. Your decision to use a weapon must be in accordance to that reality.

— 10 —

Real World

Martial arts study for self-defense only is selling short the nature of the training. Not only are you disregarding all the other benefits, but self-defense extends far beyond just kicking and punching. Physical techniques are to the totality of self-defense what four tires are to a car—important, but not the whole. Without the car, tires are nothing but something to hang from a tree for children to play on. In the case of self-defense, however, what you have left is a dangerous toy.

Violence is never just about physical technique. Nor is it limited to other issues that you pick and choose as you consider only those you believe to be germane to "real fighting." The problems are far larger and more complex. That is why these extra complications are often dismissed outright, glossed over, or simplified to the point of uselessness. Without a working knowledge of these issues, you do not have a complete grasp of what is involved in either the martial arts or self-defense. This creates some unsafe misconceptions about both. These erroneous beliefs, no matter how well you think you are being trained, will not be obvious until it is too late.

Before you even consider using your martial art for self-defense, you must be aware of two fundamental problems: it works; it doesn't work. Unfortunately, we're not being flip when we say these are both major problems.

Self-Defense versus Fighting

Let's start out optimistically and assume your martial arts training works in a self-defense situation. On this subject, we have some great news. Despite extensive arguments on martial arts forums and sales pitches from instructors trying to get you to sign up for their schools, one simple fact remains: any martial art can be used for effective self-defense.

Your martial art can protect you as you exit a situation. You can use any style's block as a shield while you get away. A simple strategy of blocking and shooting an elbow as you run can get you out of all kinds of trouble. This non-macho approach is not particularly glorious, nor does it gratify one's ego. It is, however, a very effective and proven self-defense strategy against a wide variety of threats.

Although martial arts contain elements of offense as well as self-defense, focusing on offensive fighting alone can lead to problems outside of the training hall. To be a complete martial artist you must practice both offensive and defensive techniques. It is also advisable to cross-train, even if only sparring with practitioners from different systems or arts.

Many contemporary, so-called martial arts are not fighting styles, they are training styles. They do not "teach you to fight," they train you how to move your body. Just because you know how to move your body doesn't mean you know how to fight. If that were true, both ballerinas and football players would be great fighters. More to the point, sparring is not fighting. Nor is stepping into the sports ring. In a "real fight," there are no judges or rules to protect the participants. There are no illegal moves. Whoever is still standing is the winner. The loser is probably hurt and doesn't remember a thing or is dead!

While this may sound all kinds of exciting and macho, remember that at least half the people involved in fights lose. That means, despite all your training, there is a 50/50 chance that you will be the person on the ground.

The reason you should leave fighting offensively behind at the training hall or tournament boils down to the undeniable fact about using your martial arts training on another human being: self-defense is legal; fighting is illegal.

Self-defense is doing what you must do to prevent yourself from being harmed when unjustly attacked. Walking down the street and defending yourself when someone unexpectedly jumps out of the shadows to attack you would be self-defense. Fighting, on the other hand, is your active engagement in an extended, aggressive, and, most importantly, consensual alter-cation. When an argument escalates into an exchange of blows, it is not self-defense—it's a fight. It's a fight even though both participants claim it was self-defense. Both will go to jail, and both will end up in court.

These are overly simplistic examples that are subject to the many caveats, exceptions, and extenuating circumstances that can only be sorted out in a court of law. But they do show the basic difference between self-defense and fighting.

Legal Problems of Fighting

This difference between fighting and self-defense is built into legal definitions in every state. Why is knowing this difference important? Because violence always has an aftermath. Your actions in a violent episode will affect that outcome.

The bottom line is, if you are fighting, you are part of the problem. In the aftermath, you will be treated accordingly by the legal system. No matter what you thought you were doing, your behavior prior to, during, and after the altercation will be considered and judged in this light. Even if you win the physical altercation, if you are found to have crossed certain lines, you will lose in a court of law.

To "win" a violent encounter, you must come out ahead on four different levels—not just one or two, but all four: (1) overcoming your fear and performing, (2) defeating the attacker, (3) avoiding criminal prosecution, and (4) winning in civil court if you are sued by your attacker for injuring him. Coming out ahead is a big enough challenge if you were defending yourself. If you were fighting, it is impossible.

Passing these four criteria requires much more than just knowing a deadly fighting art. It requires self-control, knowledge, and awareness of things beyond the physical act of punching someone correctly.

Here are a few very basic guidelines to tell when it crosses the line from self-defense into something illegal.

You or your student become the aggressor if:

- You were an active participant in the creation and escalation of the conflict, (for example, you were in an argument that turned into an extended punch-out).
- You did not stop attacking after the immediate threat had passed (for example, he was trying to disengage or had fallen and you kept on attacking).
- Your response was excessive beyond the threat offered (for example, you knifed someone who merely punched you).

These three standards are far more a reality than what you will hear discussed in martial arts circles about what works in a "real fight." Once these lines are crossed, it's not self-defense anymore, even if it started out as such.

Focusing on offensive fighting alone is a recipe for violating any and all of those three guidelines.

A unifying concept is the unstated assumption—by both teacher and student—that the martial artist will always be right "if he ever had to use this." This presumption of innocence of participation and instigation is not shared by our legal system. An overwhelming amount of violence could be avoided if someone simply overrides ego, apologizes, and walks away. As such, if the martial artist's behavior does not conform to legal self-defense standards, he will be prosecuted as an aggressor.

The misconception that the student will always be legally defending himself or herself is encouraged when everything is phrased in terms of self-defense in the school. You can hear the self-defense claim even when what is being taught and encouraged is anything but self-defense.

One of the authors actually witnessed a neck break from behind being taught as self-defense. That is not a self-defense move; it is a martial technique for killing. It is a combat-level move that is indefensible in court. You can play all kinds of "what if" games, but you will be hard-pressed to come up with a credible scenario where it is justified to snap someone's neck from behind while he is helpless on the ground.

Unfortunately, the current emphasis on extreme and reality-based training systems, ability to fight at any range, weapon system training, and countless other fads and marketing schemes encourage crossing the line between self-defense and fighting. These systems instill physical reactions that are not effective self-defense and would be viewed as fighting moves by the authorities. What's worse, they don't encourage a self-defense attitude (i.e., block, strike, and run). Instead, they focus on staying and engaging an opponent (a.k.a. fighting).

The nature of this training makes it far more likely the student will cross the lines into illegal behavior. We say this because error-riddled systems often try to patch their shortcomings with extreme aggressiveness. It is almost as though they were saying, "Don't fix the holes in what you are doing, just do it harder!" Whether this extra force comes from an aggressive attitude, belief in the invincibility of the fighting style, an over-reliance on being in peak physical condition, or a combination of all depends on the system. What doesn't change is the grim reality that excessive use of force is often the result of attempting to compel error-riddled techniques to work.

What is sad is that many of these schools are sincerely trying to do error detection on the traditional martial arts. They end up, however, trying to fix problems that they don't understand. As martial artists often patch techniques with muscle and speed, many "reality-based fighting systems" try to mend errors in self-defense with aggressiveness, overkill, and "deadly fighting moves." Many of the solutions currently advocated not only fail to solve the errors, but are flat-out illegal.

Unfortunately, self-defense is one of the cornerstones of martial arts marketing. You will be hard-pressed to find a school that does not promote itself as being able to teach you self-defense. What's worse is how often schools that claim to focus on self-defense are, in fact, teaching fighting.

It is incumbent on all martial arts instructors, especially those who claim to teach an art that is good for self-defense or a weapons art, to take training in the legal use of force. This does not mean simply talking to a student who also happens to be a lawyer in the dressing room. Honest instructors should actually attend classes/seminars/training. Fortunately, classes on judicious use of lethal force do exist in the handgun/shooting world and are readily available. Take this information and review your program against the standards taught there.

Misconceptions about the Martial Arts

Those are the problems you will face if your martial art style works for self-defense. Let's now turn our attention to what happens when it doesn't. This is a problem that is a very real possibility. There is no sure thing in life; your martial arts training is not a guarantee of success. We say this because, along with the host of errors we have discussed in the book, further complications arise when they are combined with the fear and the adrenaline rush of a physical attack by a person intent on causing you harm, but to an unknown degree.

The previous sentence is not only long and clumsy, but it sounds redundant. After all, if someone is attacking you, they mean you harm, right? Not necessarily. That part about "intent on causing you harm, but to an unknown degree" is an important qualifier and serious complication. As martial artists, we are regularly physically attacked by fellow students, sparring partners, and at tournaments. So why is being attacked "for real" so different?

The reasons are legion.

Most of the misconceptions regarding the effectiveness of so-called martial arts arise from student and instructor ignorance of the diversity of violence. Violence happens in a wide spectrum of ways. Traditional martial arts are insufficient to handle many of these methods. We make this statement from experience. The authors' dealings with violence range from street fights, bouncing, martial arts tournaments, and private contracting to war-time combat. We can speak from firsthand experience when we say that violence comes in many degrees and forms.

What many martial artists do not realize is that "fighting" is a very small slice of all the possible ways violence occurs. It is impossible to train for and defeat every single aspect. Most of them are predicated in making sure you can't fight back. Many years ago, one of the authors heard: "A bully doesn't want to fight you. In fact, a bully doesn't want to fight at all. He wants to beat you up and be done with it."

Despite the emphasis in some modern martial arts training to stand and engage an opponent until he is defeated, that is not how most violence occurs. Most people who use violence to achieve their ends have no desire to stand and duke it out with you, *mano a mano*, until the best man wins.

In fact, if he thinks you are capable of beating him, he will do everything in his power to make sure you never get a chance to fight. This can range from finding an easier victim, to setting an ambush, to striking first before you are prepared, to bringing along four friends, to just shooting you in the back. It all depends on how bad he wants you or what you have. If he attacks, odds are he has something up his sleeve that he feels will ensure a victory. If he gets a chance to deploy it, most likely he will.

While there is a good possibility that you can deflect the first offense, trying to stand and fight only increases his chances of success with the second, third, or fourth attack. Remember, you're not just facing a single attack. You are facing an entire offense of unknown degree. This is why we emphasize the deflect-and-run aspect of self-defense. You don't want to stay there to find out which version of violence he is intent on using. As one of the authors is fond of saying, "It's hard to get shot, stabbed, raped, robbed, or murdered if you aren't there." On top of that small detail, deflect and flee is a strategy that works with your instincts when faced with unexpected aggression.

A closely related problem is the assumption that martial artists will have time to psych themselves up to use their training.

It is no small issue. Many people have an ingrained resistance to using violence on another human. Overcoming this resistance is not something that happens easily or quickly. (Why do you think the military spends so much time and money training this resistance out of soldiers?) Having said this, attackers have overcome this resistance to varying degrees.

This allows an attacker to hit faster and with less hesitation. It may look like the attack came out of nowhere to the average person, but this is not true. The attacker has already made the mental jump that allows him to use violence. He made that jump before his victim did, which gives him a tremendous advantage.

Quite frankly, most acts of violence are over before the victim has a chance to mentally prepare himself, much less prepare an effective defense. This inability to effectively react is why the aggressor is most often the winner. It isn't due to superior fighting skills, it's because his victim is caught off guard. The victim is never allowed to regain his equilibrium, much less mount an effective defense. Forget creating a workable counteroffensive; because of the element of surprise he can't even create a defense that will work against the incessant pressing attacks by the mentally prepared antagonist.

When self-defense situations occur without your having time to mentally prepare, and combine with error-laden training that allows the attacks to get through, it turns into an overwhelming handicap if you attempt to stay and fight off an attacker.

Many people assume that all of this falls under the heading of adrenal stress: your body's natural reactions to an intense adrenaline surge; issues such as tunnel vision, auditory exclusion, time distortion, nausea, loss of bladder/bowel control, and so forth. Unfortunately, no. Although closely related, adrenal stress is an additional complication with which you must contend.

These are just a few of the reasons why martial arts may fail when someone tries to use them to fight. While you may not believe that this was a short chapter, rest assured that what we have presented is nothing more than a taste of what is involved in violence. Each of these ideas has volumes written about it. There are entire fields dedicated to understanding these issues and professions dedicated to working with them. These professions include law enforcement, psychiatry, and criminology, to say nothing of the military and legal fields.

With this in mind, you must reset your priorities from "winning" a fight to not losing a self-defense situation. This is a small, seemingly subtle difference, but one of immense importance. In closing this chapter, we would like to leave you with the wisdom of "he of the worthless opinion."

"The best way for the martial artist to survive is simply not to lose! If we focus on winning, we place expectations on ourselves that can induce unnecessary tension. The desire to win also tends to make us the aggressor, and this aggressiveness can easily lead to mistakes in our efforts to win. A dead hero is not on our agenda or goal.

"Conversely, if our sole objective is not to lose, we can unleash an indomitable spirit that is unencumbered by anxiety, heroic expectation, and the pressure to succeed. Instead, our mind and body are free to react naturally and instinctively . . . guided by our training. Experienced, we are more likely to prevail.

"When you are trying too hard to win, you will be inclined to take unnecessary risks in your determination to defeat your opponent. But when you are, instead, dedicated to not losing the encounter, you have the luxury of waiting for your opponent to make a mistake that you can exploit to achieve victory."

Afterword

When we first come to the martial arts, we approach with a sense of wonder and a thirst for knowledge. We tend to lose that awe as the arts become an everyday part of our lives. We often reach a level of comfort with what we know and tend to hit training and learning plateaus.

It is important to recognize the nature of these stages. People often mistake them as reaching the top of the mountain, but they are simply levels in our learning where things stabilize for a time. Growing and reaching plateaus are intrinsic parts of martial arts development, just as movement and rest are part of a journey. The problem arises if our rest becomes permanent and we don't continue the journey.

At first, plateaus are comfortable resting spots. In time, however, we discover that stabilization means we have stopped growing and learning. Getting off a plateau can be as much work as getting on it. At this point what you do is significant. You can continue to grow or you can stagnate or quit the martial arts altogether. We need to look closely at these last two choices because they don't have to happen.

Quitting is common. How many of the people you started with are still in the martial arts? They usually fade away, finding other hobbies and interests and pursuing them. Boredom is often one reason for dropping the arts. Amazingly enough, the highest per capita dropout rate appears to be among black belts. When you look at percentages in commercial schools, the black belt turnover rate is just as high—if not higher—than lower belts.

We admit the trend in commercial schools to abuse newly minted black belts by using them as a free teaching workforce is a significant factor in this loss. That is a business practice disguised as a martial art tradition. The right or wrong of it is beyond the scope of this book. Our concern is with an individual's growth in martial arts understanding.

The tendency of a student to drift away after achieving a black belt takes on a different significance when viewed in the context of plateaus. This is especially true if the student came up through the ranks thinking that a black belt was the top of the mountain. If getting that belt was the motivating goal, there isn't much left after it is achieved. Although lip service is often paid to deeper meanings of the black belt, the sole objective has been to achieve that coveted symbol. That rank, rather than understanding, is the goal.

It is small wonder that, upon reaching this plateau, people eventually drift away. They've done it, now what? Where does the new black belt go from here? What is before him on this mountain peak? An endless stream of teaching the same limited understanding of a system?

Although the black belt is sign of accomplishment, that accomplishment is having reached a plateau with a firm knowledge and understanding of the fundamentals and basics of the art. A black belt is not a sign of mastery; it is at this level that you should be capable of learning more of the bunkai. To correctly learn these internal moves within the kata, you must have a well-rooted foundation of knowledge. In the scramble for degrees, nobody notices that this approach keeps the black belt as a paying student, and at a status that, no matter how far he or she advances, will ever equal the master, much less surpass him.

Unfortunately, plateaus are not exclusively limited to students. Many paper masters have plateaued and stayed there. When this happens, the so-called deeper truths they teach are, in fact, of the same quality as the information that has been relayed since Day 1. It's not deeper, it's just different versions of the same thing. It is the same level—not a deeper understanding—simply applied to different things.

A major problem arises when the student reaches the plateau that the instructor has leveled out on. Unfortunately, this is easy to do with the current trend of rank inflation, i.e., 21-year-old masters, 30-year-old grand masters, "masters" in five or six different styles and black belts guaranteed within a year. Sad to say, we are not making up any of these examples. Even someone who has been doing martial arts for many years may have plateaued at a level easily reached by an eager student.

There are many schools that exploit that process. Often we see instructors who have jumped from one, two, three straight to ten, overwhelming students with a series of dan rankings rather than details four, five, six, seven, eight, and nine.

Many schools, in the name of keeping students interested, continually pack on more and more techniques. These techniques often are taken from other systems without a full understanding of the body mechanics of that art.

What does this really create? Does a shallow knowledge of hundreds of techniques really instill depth of understanding? Or does it just become a never-ending stream of poorly understood information? There are some people who thrive in this environment. Their challenge is not to become better at what they do, but instead be the one who has the biggest collection of techniques.

What often happens in this situation is that people fail to refine what they already know before adding these new things. They don't understand what they know, but they keep adding to it. This leaves them with a cartoon understanding of what they are doing. Unless you specifically focus on refining the fundamentals of a technique—and by doing so, plumbing its depths—this cartoon version will be the extent of people's understanding. No matter how many more techniques you add, people get bored on a constant diet of watching cartoons.

Plateaus are levels of understanding, not volume. You can have a very big plateau, one made wider by knowledge of many techniques—-but it is still a plateau. These stalling points occur when you have gone as far as you can by thinking a certain way or the requisite skill has not yet been absorbed into the motion of the body. It is one thing to understand the next level, it is another to be ready to perform it comfortably. Some people think plateaus are walls. By persisting with a certain viewpoint, you will run into a wall that you cannot overcome, no matter how many more techniques you add to your repertoire.

You overcome these walls or get off these plateaus by returning to the fundamentals. By reexamining those things you think you know with an experienced perspective that you didn't have when you first learned them, your understanding will literally explode exponentially. Often you must reexamine these ideas outside the context of your own system. Cross-training can be an incredibly valuable asset, especially if you learn a system that is radically different than the one you already know, such as a soft style if you are a hard stylist. In any case, it is important to get input from sources outside your regular circle. Often such close-knit groups tend to be self-reinforcing and of a single mind. What you are looking for is a different perspective on the fundamentals.

In one of the author's schools, the attitude about a black belt is it is like a degree from any other institution. It doesn't mean you have the answers, it means you now are qualified to work toward understanding the larger questions. Early on, students are told that their goal is not the black belt, but rather the search for understanding and growth.

As instructors, it is our task to show students not only the breadth, but also the depth of the martial arts. This means that we must set the example for this ongoing search for depth and understanding. If you have lost your excitement, your thirst for knowledge and the ongoing search for understanding, how can you expect to keep students interested?

If all you keep feeding them are shallow interpretations based on poor understanding (or fabricated reasons), you're going to lose students. The same sense of wonder, excitement of learning, experience of growth, and exhilaration of the challenge the arts provide that first appealed to them upon entering the martial arts will evaporate. Those who stay will do so for reasons other than learning, which brings us to the next point.

Another common route when one reaches a plateau is stagnation. This comes in many ways, most not really related to the martial arts at all, but related instead to human behavior. How many people have you encountered who use martial arts for social purposes? Or use their rank to build their egos? Every few years they advance in rank, but do they really grow as martial artists? Are they increasing their understanding or perfecting their art, or are they just doing the same things over and over again and calling themselves better? It's not difficult to plumb the shallows of these instructors' understanding. Often when the well runs dry, instead of digging deeper, they try to widen it by collecting more and more stuff—patching it onto their existing system to stay ahead of their students. This also is where the grandiose claims of paper masters begin.

When this occurs, it is no longer about the martial arts. It is, instead, about business, ego, and cults of personality. Although these are the source of many of the problems that plague the modern martial arts, addressing them is beyond the scope of this book. We can say, however, that research into these topics will shed some interesting light on the behavior one often encounters in dojo politics.

We do not mean to sound critical of the martial arts. Growth in the arts is difficult enough without these extra road-blocks a person will encounter—not *could*, mind you, but *will*.

What about the person seeking to reach greater depths of understanding? How does he handle these plateaus? He must first accept the fact that growth in the martial arts is a series of plateaus that often are very frustrating. You hit walls that you can't see, define, or overcome. What's worse is not knowing what is wrong, but knowing something isn't right.

This is the natural process of growth in the arts and can happen to anyone. Maybe sooner for some, later for others, but many of us will encounter it. How we deal with these plateaus determines whether we grow or not, whether we stay with the martial arts or leave, or whether we fall into our own pride, stop learning, and become a paper master.

This also can become a trap, creating a constant seeker of the ultimate martial art. Often such people quit one school and move to another that has a different emphasis or style. This is called "cross-training" by those who do it and "quitting" by so-called masters, who want students to stay and continue paying them money.

The truth is that the further you advance in the martial arts, the harder it is to find someone who can help you break free of these plateaus. In the beginning, when you know nothing, there are numerous people who know more. As you advance, you find countless people stuck on the same plateaus, and there is a lot of lateral, not upward, movement trying to find ways off these plateaus—especially among the higher ranks.

What few realize is that there is a way to break free. That is to remain a student, always growing in depth and understanding.

Since the path to perfection is ongoing, there are always new depths to discover, different ways to refine your skills, new and exciting challenges and things to learn—not only in your style, but in that of others. To do this, you must always return to the fundamentals. What is it that makes this move work? What must be there?

One of the author's school symbols is rice stalks that curl back in looping circles. There is wisdom in that simple symbol. As he often points out, the path of the martial arts is like these heavily laden rice stalks. The more grains of rice on the stalk, the more it bends down to its beginning. Whereas a stalk with only a few grains stands straight up. A field of bountiful rice bows down low, returning to its roots. A field that is scarce in value reaches highest. It is this height that seems most impressive to the uninformed.

Knowing 27 different blocks does you no good if none can meet the goal of "don't get hit" because all lack the fundamentals. The question isn't how well do you do the style. It is how well does what you do meet the fundamentals and goals underlying a specific action. Does a block keep you from getting hit?

Does a blow deliver force into your opponent? If not, then odds are the problem is related to missing fundamentals.

Plateaus may occur when we have taken a certain manner of thinking to its height. That does not mean we can go no higher, but we cannot do that with the same kind of thinking. Albert Einstein once said, "We cannot solve our problems with the same thinking we used when we created them." This is why we must return to the fundamentals. We must backtrack down the path that led to the plateau where we're stuck. With everything we have learned on that path, we must review the fundamentals to find significance that we overlooked, didn't understand, or just couldn't see before. From this new perspective on the fundamentals, look to see what other paths arise and follow them. Experiment and test the knowledge on these new paths. Because each path has different significance, information, and interpretation, each will teach you something different. Every time you return to the fundamentals after pursuing a path, what you will have learned on that path will reveal to you new meanings and depths in the fundamentals.

The fundamentals are the roots of the martial art, but you cannot grow deep roots without nourishing them. You must constantly return to these if you want to grow. The more you return to these roots—those things that make it work—the greater the bounty of your field. The more options, pathways, variations (or whatever you want to call them) you will see arising from the fundamentals. Often you will become so involved in investigating these options that you won't even notice you have gotten off the plateau.

The deeper your understanding of these fundamentals, the more effective you will be. This is because you will know why such things as elbow placement and weight transfer are critical for a move's success, and that is what you will work toward perfecting. When you understand this, you will not only make sure these elements are present, but seek to refine them.

The path of the martial arts is one of subtlety.

That simple statement can redefine your study of the arts. It is achieving the same results with less energy. It is refining your skills to the point where instead of having to move a foot, you need only an inch. For the subtle to work, all the fundamentals must be present and honed. We have attempted to help you identify some of them so you can see how to first apply and then refine them—in whatever style you study.

As we said at the beginning of this book, it is not our intention to tell you the right way to do the martial arts. What we hopefully have done is help the martial artist reexamine what he or she is doing and—more importantly—what they have been taught, as well as teach. This is intended to help the student continue to grow both within the martial arts and within himself by returning to the fundamentals to discover all the different ways they can manifest.

In doing so, we hope to help you rediscover the exciting and wonderful possibilities that the martial arts offer, as well as the sheer joy of learning.

We wish you well on your journey.

Index

Index

Index